PACK UP AND PAINT

with Oils

Tom Robb

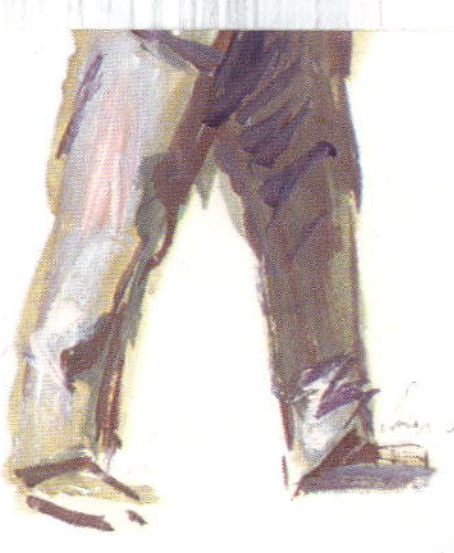

COLLINS

First published in 1986
by William Collins Sons & Co Ltd
London. Glasgow. Sydney
Auckland. Johannesburg

© Phoebe Phillips Editions, 1986

Designed and produced by PHOEBE PHILLIPS EDITIONS

British Library Cataloguing in Publication Data

Robb, Tom
    Pack up and paint with oils.
    (Pack up and paint series)
    1. Polymer painting – Technique
    I. Title
    751.42'6   ND1535

ISBN 0-00-412126-0

ISBN 0 00 412128 7 (Watercolour)
0 00 412126 0 (Oils)
0 00 412127 9 (Pack Up & Sketch)

Printed and bound in Belgium by
Offset-Printing van den Bossche N.V.

Introduction

While sketches and watercolours were traditionally done out of doors, oil has always been the serious medium, worked on carefully by the artist and often by apprentices and helpers, in the workshop or studio, the picture built up by many layers of thin paint, glaze on top of glaze.

Suddenly, in the mid-19th century, all that changed, thanks largely to the Impressionists. They wanted to give their paintings a reality that was possible only when the scene was painted from life. Their canvases glowed with the sunlight, air and pure colour caught and held in the landscapes and riverscapes around Paris and along the rural Seine.

This revolutionary change of scene has benefited us all ever since. We may not subscribe to their theories about colour and light; we may not choose to paint in the style we have come to associate with them; but few landscape painters today would deny that working out of doors is the most compelling and deeply satisfying method of keeping in constant touch with their surroundings.

Learning to make the most of your time out of doors is a skill like any other. Painting in oils involves carrying a great deal of equipment, and it will take both careful organization and a deep-felt commitment to use your time productively as well as enjoyably. I hope that both pleasure and achievement will be enhanced by this handbook.

Tom Robb

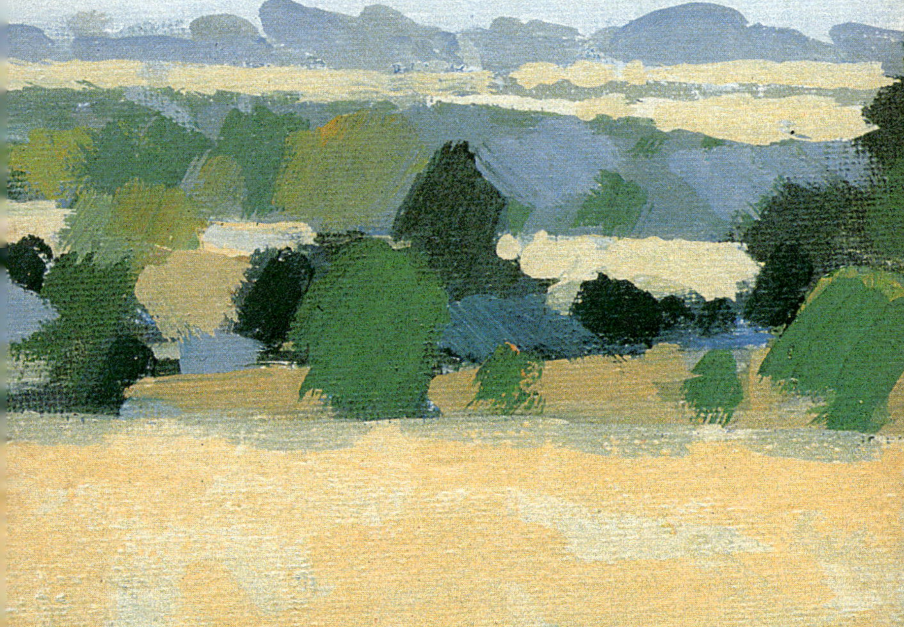

Contents

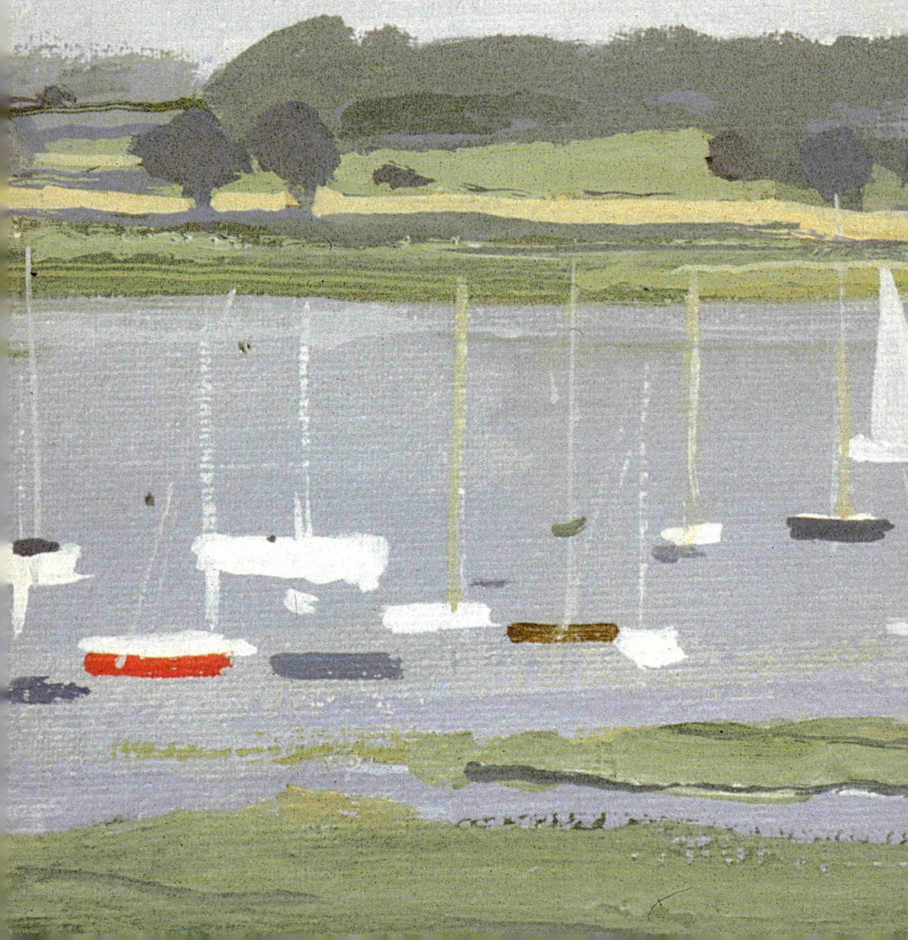

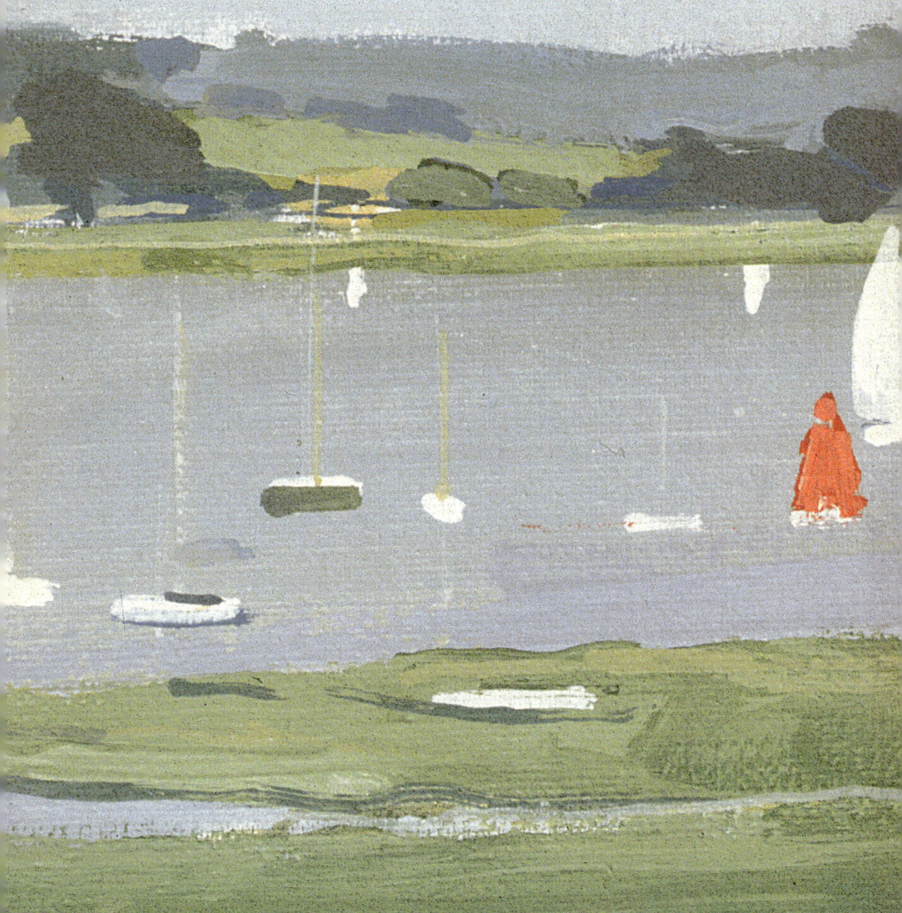

Why?

The two questions almost never asked, and certainly the hardest to answer: why are you packing up to go out and paint? Why are you spending time, money and effort to learn what to do and how to do it without knowing why you are doing it?

Through all the years that I have been a professional artist, a teacher and an adviser to countless students and would-be students of all ages, it has been startling to discover that these fundamental queries are missing from books, from classrooms, and even from conversations. Yet without a perceptive look into your own motives and needs, whatever you achieve will be less than you are capable of, and ultimately less rewarding.

So I have put down here the three basic approaches that anyone can make to painting. It matters not at all which one you feel is right for you. It matters only that you understand what you choose, and why you may change in the future.

For someone who is looking for simple enjoyment, for heightened awareness of beauty through art, and for the sheer delight of being out in the open air with something interesting to do, my advice would be to ignore most of the detailed instructions. Take a box of paints, brushes, a canvas board, turpentine and a rag for wiping the brushes. Pack a good lunch and a bottle of wine, and let the paintings happen. Use the information we give you to take the fuss and bother out of colour mixing. At the end of the day you will be able to take pleasure home with you in the form of a painting that is only for yourself – a memento of a magic afternoon, a reminder of an incredible sunset. That is rationale enough for any human being.

A second approach is usually the result of some years of learning, either on your own or in art classes. Having already attained a certain standard, you may be anxious to learn new ideas and perceptions as well as to increase your basic vocabulary of skills.

Your primary lesson would be an appreciation that painting can be more than recording what you see. It is demanding intellectually and even physically. It is learning to take a structured approach so that you can get greater satisfaction out of the actual experience of painting, and the artist's way of looking at the world. You need to ask yourself each time you set out what you want to achieve that day. Instead of throwing a few things in a bag the night before (and hoping you'll find a landscape in a bag when you get home) you should be sitting down and planning your trip, thinking about your ideas and how to programme yourself – the kind of 'psyching up' that is now so much a part of competitive sports. But this is not to win as such, but to force your precious time to work for you. The handbooks in the *Pack Up and Paint* series offer a ritual which can be used as a lens to get yourself into focus: looking over your equipment and setting it out; going through the five basics; trying to match some of the colour code mixtures for yourself. And each time you return from a trip with the landscape you intended to make, you will hang it up with a double satisfaction -- both from the painting itself, and from knowing how you achieved it.

The third approach to painting is one that is almost never mentioned, even to advanced students, and yet it is fundamental to the life of any artist. After you have been working for some time, you should ask yourself which you really enjoy: the act of painting or the expression of yourself, which might be just as rewarding in another direction. Beyond this stage, painting is not necessarily enjoyable, and seldom entirely satisfying. It is demanding to a degree seldom recognized even in art schools.

If you want to be an artist in the full sense of the word, then it will permeate every part of your life, and everything you do. But the more you actually achieve, and the more you demand of yourself, the less you will probably enjoy the process!

This is perhaps the most serious commitment you can make and it should not be made lightly. Whether you are baking a cake or writing a letter to a friend or mowing the lawn, your mind will be partly (or even wholly) occupied with thinking about the texture of flour and the colour of pastry, the kind of pen you are using and the line the ink is making on the paper – or the difficulties of painting the thousand blades of grass with one wash. Read the letters of Cézanne, Van Gogh, Matisse; throughout their lives the greatest artists were always fighting their own limitations to create with their hands what they saw so clearly in their minds. The reward for most of us is in the effort, not the achievement.

The final project in each book has been chosen to provide a fillip for the more experienced painter; utilizing their disciplines will be another way of forcing yourself to recognize where you are going, and through which form of expression you want to travel.

A final word: none of these approaches is exclusive. The most casual Sunday painter will want to do something more now and then; the most dedicated professional must take time to remember how much fun painting can be. Simply understanding what you need and want on any particular day will increase your chances of achievement and enjoyment a hundredfold.

Planning ahead

There are five basic factors to take into account whenever you plan a painting trip:

1 The time available
2 The place
3 The weather
4 The season
5 The purpose of the trip

No matter how experienced you are, and however much you think you will remember everything, it will do no harm to tack the above list up somewhere near the door, so that you remind yourself to check each answer off as you get ready.

1 The time available

It is not easy to do very quick sketches with oil in the same way that you can with pen and pencil, or even with watercolour. The canvas can be prepared beforehand, of course, and a few tubes of paint are easily carried in a small box, but unless you are

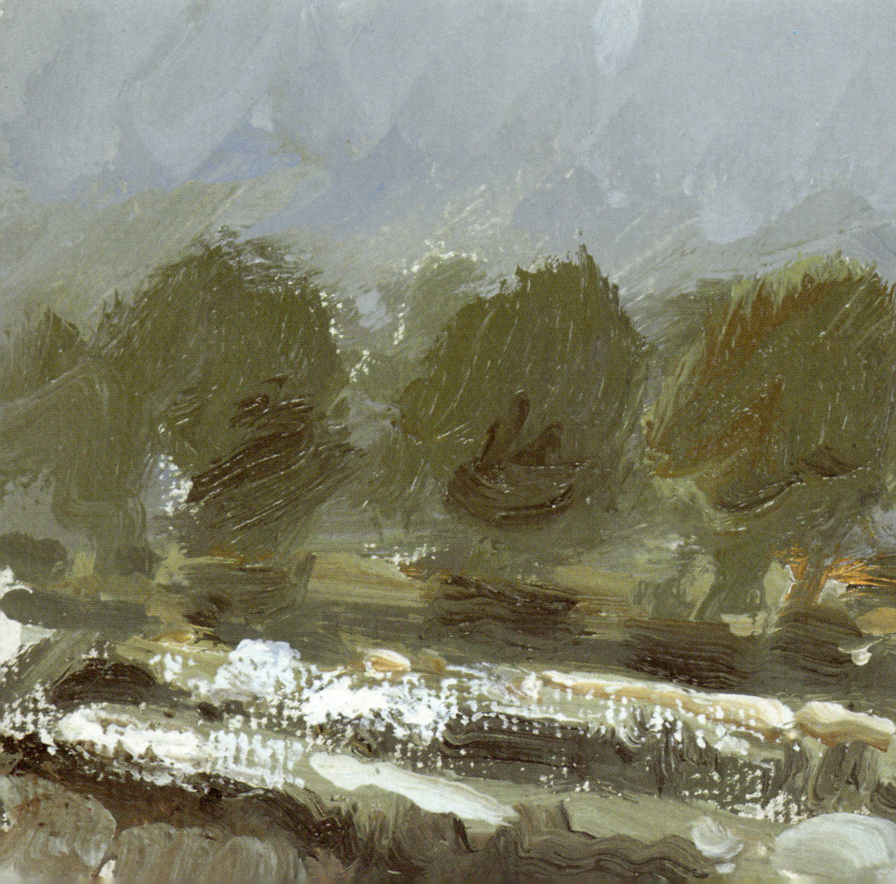

prepared to work holding the canvas at a convenient angle, you will still need an easel, and you will also need a bottle of turpentine, a jar for cleaning the brushes, a rag and a means of getting the painting home again without smudging.

I would suggest that if you can really spend only half an hour, you make some preliminary sketches, rather than attempting a finished painting. You can use oil or acrylic paint, perhaps in only one or two colours, and an oil sketching pad instead of a canvas.

Acrylic paints, if applied thinly, do dry quickly – in five minutes or so. I believe that is their chief advantage as a medium.

It is wise to accept that an excursion to paint outdoors will take you at least three or four hours; a whole day is better still, when you can break off for a cup of coffee and lunch, and still have plenty of time left to paint.

I've learned over the years that I concentrate best on oil painting during a weekend or a long holiday, when I am not rushed into working too fast, or into trying to conform to a busy schedule. After all, that is what painting is all about – tranquillity, and the calm of working thoughtfully at something you love.

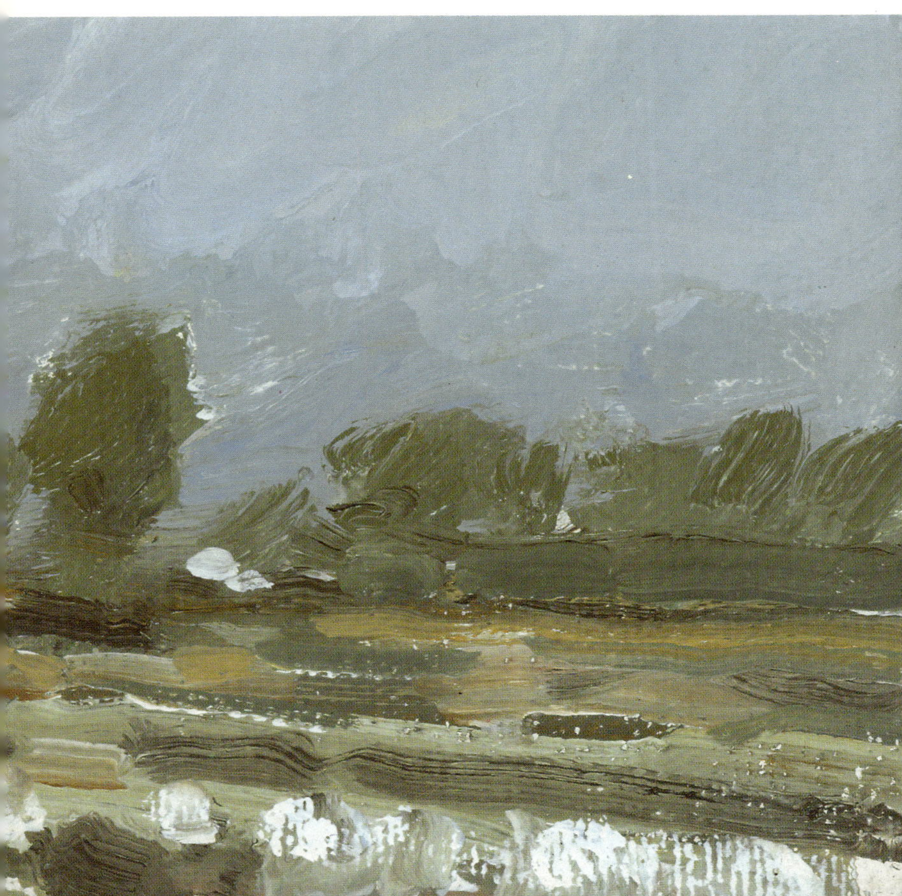

2 The place

When you are thinking about where to go, take into account the medium you will be using. The principle is to find an advantage in the good things that are available, no matter what the conditions, rather than to fight against nature – and your equipment.

Steep slopes are often attractive viewing spots, and unlike watercolours oils are quite adaptable to daunting conditions. Oil paint is thick and creamy, not runny, so it can be used at all sorts of odd angles (although I do admit I've never tried painting upside down, or under water).

So long as you can prop yourself up comfortably, and position the easel so that it is right for your hand and eye, mixing the paint is no problem.

The bottles of oil and turpentine are usually sturdy enough to be propped up too, but always remember to cap them firmly after every use instead of leaving them open as you might do on a flat surface. One slight wave of an enthusiastic hand, and a vital bottle can go tumbling over, splashing its contents in every direction.

Collapsible legs on your easel are a must, with a few stones to buttress them as needed. A stone suspended from the cross-piece will keep most easels from swaying in the kind of gusty wind that is so frequent at high altitudes.

Beaches, as always, pose their own peculiar problems. Blowing sand can turn the surface of your oil painting into a sheet of sandpaper within a minute, and you will have to scrape everything off and start again.

The seaside is fine for environmental painting – you can deliberately produce a sand picture with different colours and textures – but be wary if you want to keep the painting clean. Work inside a windbreak (the kind they sell in beach stores) and get the finished canvas under cover as quickly as possible, laying it flat inside the car or at the bottom of your empty carrying box.

Take along a flat-bottomed seat of some sort (a chair or stool with legs will sink unevenly into the sand) and a heavy box for keeping all your bits and pieces handily beside your easel.

It is difficult to clean brushes at the beach – the sand gets into everything – so make extra sure that you clean them properly when you get home; otherwise they will be unusably abrasive the next time you paint.

That goes for your palette too, and I suggest using a disposable palette pad for seaside excursions. You simply throw it away, and thus avoid the risk of carrying home sand or sharp bits of shell that can grind into your brushes.

The countryside is the real Mecca for oil painters: good views, a quiet atmosphere and, if you choose your spot well, plenty of space for all your gear.

A lightweight canvas leaf-carrier – the kind that has attached handles on all four corners – makes an ideal tablecloth on which to lay out bottles, tubes, brushes and so on, as well as to rest spare canvases before they are used.

Obviously working at table height is most convenient, and you can find small garden tables on legs that fold up; they are generally less expensive than purpose-made artist's boxes.

Using what you find is one way to put your surroundings into your work. For instance, try mixing some of the leaf mould around trees or bushes with a little turpentine, and using this as a basic size over the bottom of the primed canvas. It will convey a feeling of the predominant tones in the landscape around you, even though it is likely to get covered up quickly by layers of paint. Another suggestion: instead of using a palette knife for thick impasto areas, roll a stick over the paint to pick up texture from the bark.

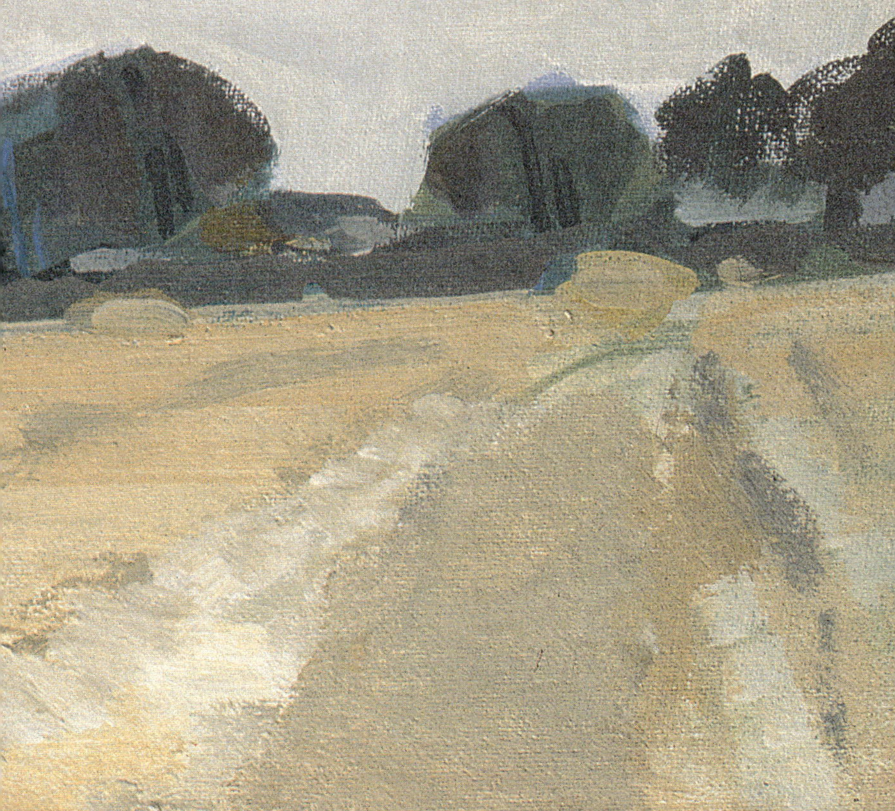

3 The weather

In general terms, the only element that makes oil painting almost impossible is a strong wind. Every bit of debris in the air will find its way onto your wet canvas, and since it may stay sticky for days – even weeks when the humidity is high – protecting your picture becomes a major priority.

The illustration on the right shows a small square of canvas with a thin coat of oil paint, which was left out near the beach for only a few hours. The amount of debris that found its way onto the picture is quite amazing.

You can, of course, make use of 'wind' painting as a kind of collage or environmental experiment. Try painting an old piece of board with oil and leaving it, on an easel, in the middle of a field. Repeat this once or twice, in a different field each time. You might find yourself with an interesting result – different kinds of flower seeds, leaves, etc. stuck to the boards.

If you are determined to paint outside in oils no matter what the conditions, carry a wind-break wherever you go. But make it easier for yourself by looking for sheltered places – the lee of a house or farm building, a porch or a conservatory with a view onto the garden.

Rain and snow, on the other hand, are not real deterrents. So long as the canvas does not become saturated, the paint will adhere to the surface; but it takes longer to dry out than the fabric, so you may well get some buckling, especially on canvas boards.

Acrylics, of course, can be diluted with water. They are not, therefore, a satisfactory substitute for oils in wet weather.

Remember to protect yourself as well as your canvas. Standing for the fairly long time a large oil painting will take, in squelchy shoes and sopping socks, cannot help your concentration. A rain hat should have a long enough flap to ensure that the water runs down the outside – not the inside – of your coat. A sailor's oilskin slicker is far more useful than a traditional artist's smock!

Sharply cold weather may make the paints stiffen in their tubes, which in turn makes it difficult to put them onto your palette. Warm each tube in your hands for a few minutes before you try to press out the pigment, otherwise it might crack, and paint will come oozing out of both ends at once.

Originally acrylic was sometimes packed in plastic tubes. These can, and do, crack open in freezing weather, so make sure any new paint you buy is in metal foil packs.

Some oils thicken considerably in cold weather, and may become slightly opaque. Try using turpentine to help the pigment flow easily and dry quickly.

Hot weather can make oils very soft, so you may need less turpentine or oil to mix them. You'll need a hat to keep the sun away from your eyes, and try neutral-density sunglasses which lower the intensity of colours without changing them. Take the glasses off from time to time to check your work.

Whatever you do, don't drop your finished oil painting in a mud puddle – if it falls on its painted surface it will be the ruin of a day's work.

Remember that a layer of acrylic, used like fairly thin oil paint, dries in about half an hour. This makes acrylic paintings easier to transport in bad weather, and allows you to wash off the mud if you do get them dirty carrying them home.

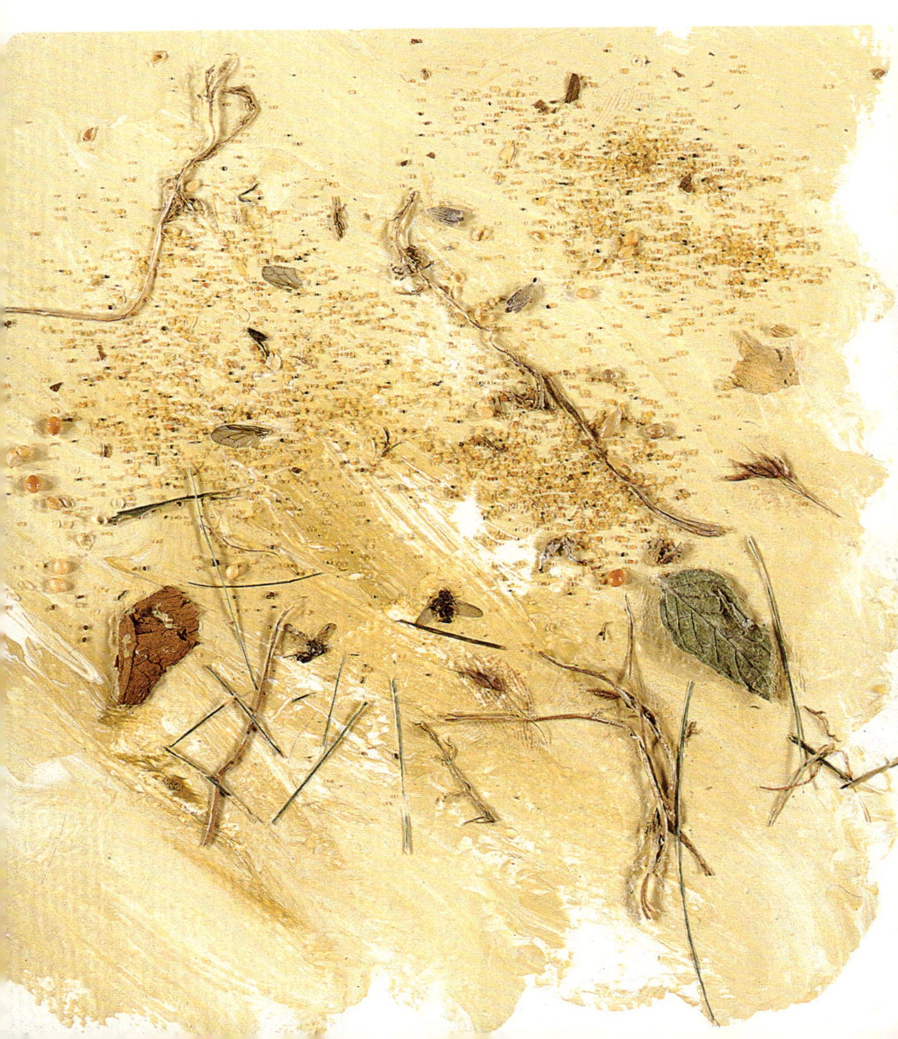

4 The season

A seasonal palette is as appropriate for oils as it is for
watercolours or pastels.

In general, the spring colours are clear and light – the yellows
like new sunlight; the blues fresh and airy; the pinks blush-
coloured rather than hot; the greens crisp as a new-budded leaf.

As the summer wears on, everything becomes deeper and
richer: the greens darker, the reds and pinks more rosy and
purple. Even in the city, the heavier atmosphere brings a weight
to the colours of shop displays. Cool the palette down where
appropriate with plenty of strong Zinc white or Titanium white.

During the autumn, all the oranges and reds flame into dramatic
brilliance, with the full-bodied textures that oil paints convey so
well. Take advantage of the medium and lay on your pure
colours with a reasonably free hand.

Finally, the winter palettes of whites, greys and blues can be
pointed up by the sparing use of Sienna brown and the darker
greens of Cobalt and Viridian.

Spring

Light green, mixed from white and Viridian green; Yellow
ochre; Lemon yellow; Light blue, mixed from Cerulean blue
and white.

Summer

Cadmium red; Cadmium yellow; warm green, mixed from
Viridian green and Cadmium yellow; Burnt umber; Cobalt
blue.

Autumn

Deep red, mixed from Cadmium red and Alizarin crimson;
Burnt sienna; Cadmium orange; Light blue, mixed from
Ultramarine blue and white.

Winter

Dark blue, mixed from Prussian blue and white; black; greys,
mixed from Ivory black and white; Light blue, mixed from
Cerulean blue and white.

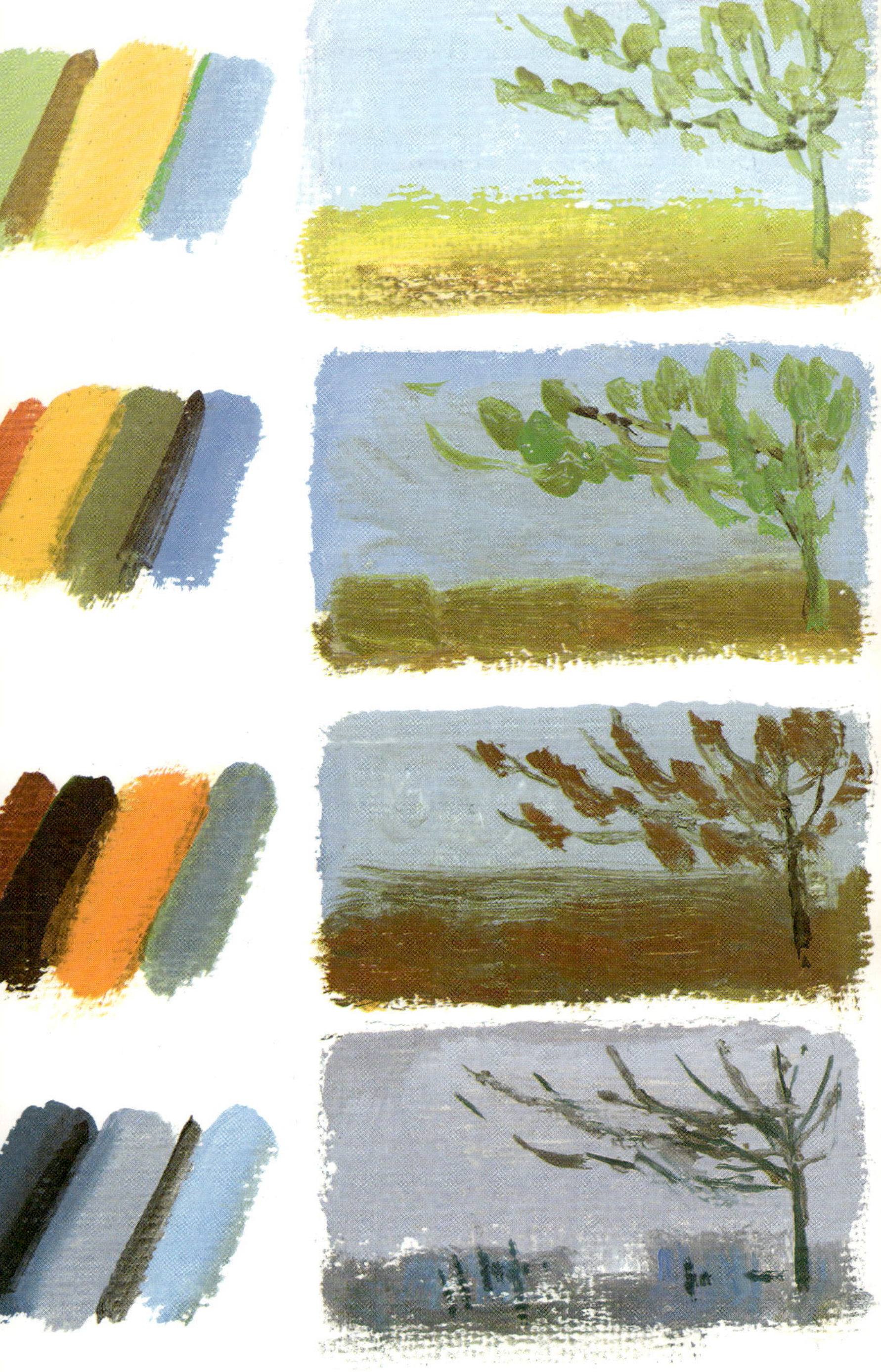

5 The purpose

When you set out to paint outdoors in oil, you are looking for a quite different landscape from the sort you choose for watercolour or drawing. For one thing, you are involved in a three-dimensional medium; even quite flat oil painting, thinned into wash, has a depth that is missing in the other mediums. If you use oil in the normal way, the brush marks, the ridges and the valleys catch the light and hold the colour in a unique way.

Your oil painting should be conditioned by the fact that oil paint becomes the object you are painting, not a picture of it. Think of a well-known Van Gogh landscape – his field of wheat with a red cart, so vivid you can almost reach out and touch it, even though the painting is far from realistic in the usual sense.

Oil paintings have direction as well as depth, often giving three or four sweeping tones of colour from one pigment. An understanding of the medium's basic nature is essential to every decision you make about shape, colour, content and style.

The mood of your landscape should be reflected in the tools you use. A cool, calm evening will look best with long, easy strokes, thin washes and glazes, clear, quiet colours. A stormy sea or a lowering sky and violent wind should be put down with a rough brush or a palette knife.

You can paint with bravura and speed, covering the canvas quickly and depending on inspiration rather than consideration, or you can work slowly and carefully, planning wash upon wash, glaze upon glaze, until the picture emerges. Working over the entire canvas at once is a style that allows you to see what is happening to the overall view, and lets you take advantage of the fact that changes in light and shadow will be reflected everywhere in the picture.

Or you can draw in the outline with a pale blue-grey wash (I never use charcoal for underdrawing – it always shows through in the end) and then work systematically from one side of the painting to the other, filling in as you go, and finishing when you reach the other side!

All of these approaches will be present in some degree no matter what you do, but by clearing your mind and planning to emphasize one or the other, you will give yourself a greater freedom to concentrate and to produce satisfactory work. And at the end of the day, you'll find yourself with a painting that says as much about yourself as it does about the landscape.

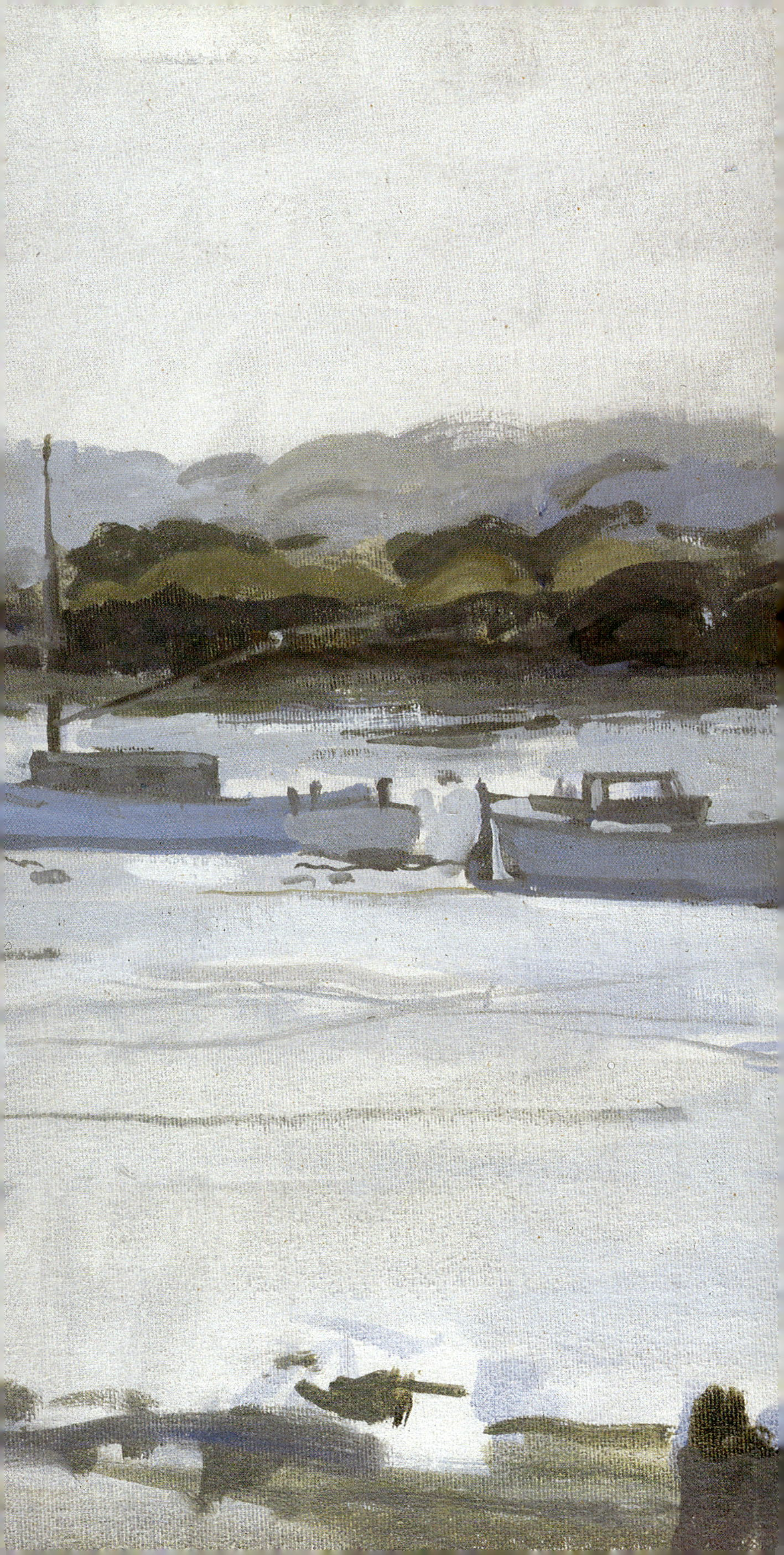

Packing up to go out

Oil painting has always been treated as a major exercise in logistics. By the time you have considered all the bits and pieces you think you need, it can seem almost too much of a problem to go out, much less to assemble everything you want.

This unfortunate attitude was responsible for keeping oil painters closeted in their studios for generations until the Impressionist painters showed how easy it was and how much could be gained by being *en plein air* with the whole world in front of you as a subject for your canvas.

The painting on the title page is an adaptation of a well-known photograph of Cézanne with his easel strapped to his back, and all his gear comfortably carried.

So think about the five basic factors I've mentioned: the time available; the place where you think it would be pleasant to paint; the season; the weather, and your purpose in starting out at all. After that, you have only to make certain that your tools are carefully chosen and as carefully packed – and you're on your way.

Walking

For obvious reasons you'll want to take as little as possible. This is where prepared canvas boards come into their own. They are much lighter than watercolour boards with stretched paper, and easier to carry than canvas over stretchers. Two small ones – say, 6" by 8" (153 × 203mm), or 8" by 10" (203 × 254mm) – should do nicely for a walking trip.

A handful of brushes next, and the basic tubes of paint listed for the basic palette. I prefer to carry my own small wooden palette, somewhat more colourful, as you can see, than a pad of clean tear-off palettes.

I haven't included an easel. It is possible to paint without one by propping the canvas up on your knee or on a convenient ledge. If you can manage it, however, carry a lightweight aluminium outdoor easel.

Sometimes I use an old biscuit tin for tubes and brushes, their hairs protected by rolled tubes of polythene. A small bottle of turpentine can be tucked into a corner. Finally, you will need a rag for wiping brushes and your hands.

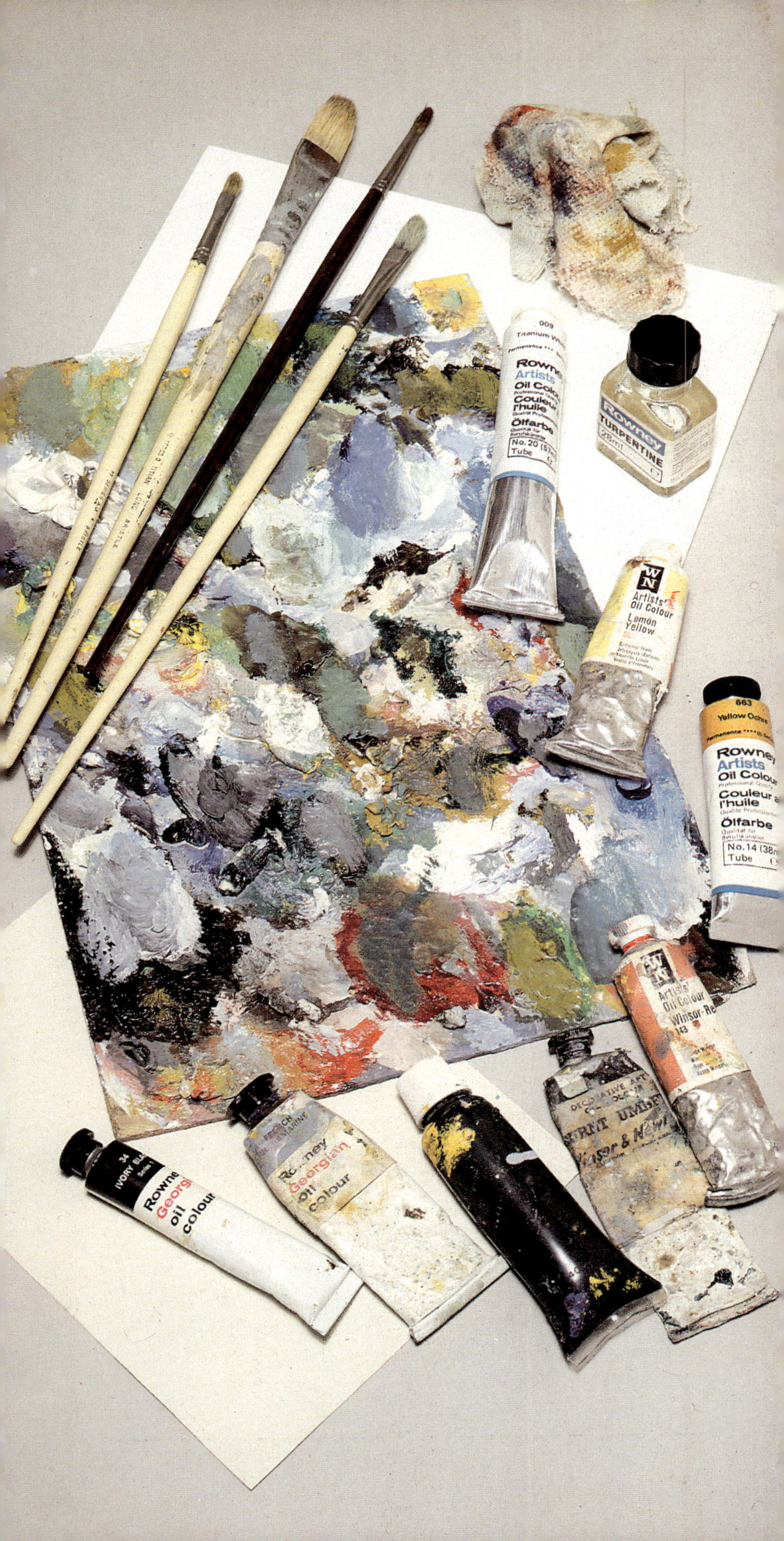

009
Titanium White
Rowney
Artists
Oil Colour
Couleur à l'huile
Ölfarbe
No. 20
Tube
Rowney
TURPENTINE
25ml
W N
Artists'
Oil Colour
Lemon Yellow
663
Yellow Ochre
Rowney
Artists
Oil Colour
Couleur à l'huile
Ölfarbe
No. 14
Tube
W N
Artists'
Oil Colour
Winsor Red
143
DECORATIVE ART
BURNT UMBER
Reeves & Newton
IVORY BLACK
34
Rowney
Georgian
oil colour
FRENCH
ULTRAMARINE
Rowney
Georgian
oil colour

With transport

Once you have some sort of transport, painting with oils becomes comfortable and convenient.

The first addition is a proper easel. Lightweight sketching ones are fine, but I prefer my old wooden travelling easel, solid enough to stay upright in all conditions, and secure enough to allow me to put on any size or weight of canvas. This goes into the back of the car, along with a fairly substantial box of colours with an extended palette, plus those few special colours I might want to add for convenience.

I don't believe you can have too many brushes, and as you can see on the right I take at least a dozen with me, and usually many more than that. There are two easels to choose from: the top of my oil-painting box, and my old easel, covered in many layers of paint, comfortable to hold and familiar as a friend. This is one of the important aspects of painting outdoors. As you get to know and appreciate good equipment, you use the same tools year after year.

If I am also going to do a great deal of sketching, perhaps making studies for a major painting or checking colours on small areas of a large canvas, I might add a pack of disposable palettes. These can take very small amounts of paint for immediate use, and can be simply torn off and thrown away when you are finished. But don't leave them lying about. Many oil paints are made with poisonous chemicals and dyes, and in any case no one appreciates litter, however artistic its origins.

A good-sized bottle of linseed oil and some turpentine go into the car next, in a box with the palette knives, scrapers and a few rags. A box of charcoal sticks is also useful. Although I prefer to use a weak blue-grey oil paint when I sketch direct onto the canvas, you may need the charcoal to help you divide up the proportions or simply to sketch the scene first on a bit of paper. The oil sketching pad I add is useful for that, and for experimenting with colour contrasts and blendings away from the canvas I'm working on.

Finally, I take an assortment of canvas-covered boards. Stretched canvas is, of course, the ideal and as bulk is no problem if you have your own transport, you may prefer to paint on this. But it is much more expensive than the prepared boards, which I find quite satisfactory for smaller pictures. However, if you do a great deal of oil painting outdoors, you may enjoy making and stretching your own canvases. You can use almost any natural material, primed in white. Although many artists prime their canvases in browns or sepias, I feel that it is impossible to achieve a clear blue sky in landscape with a darker undercoat.

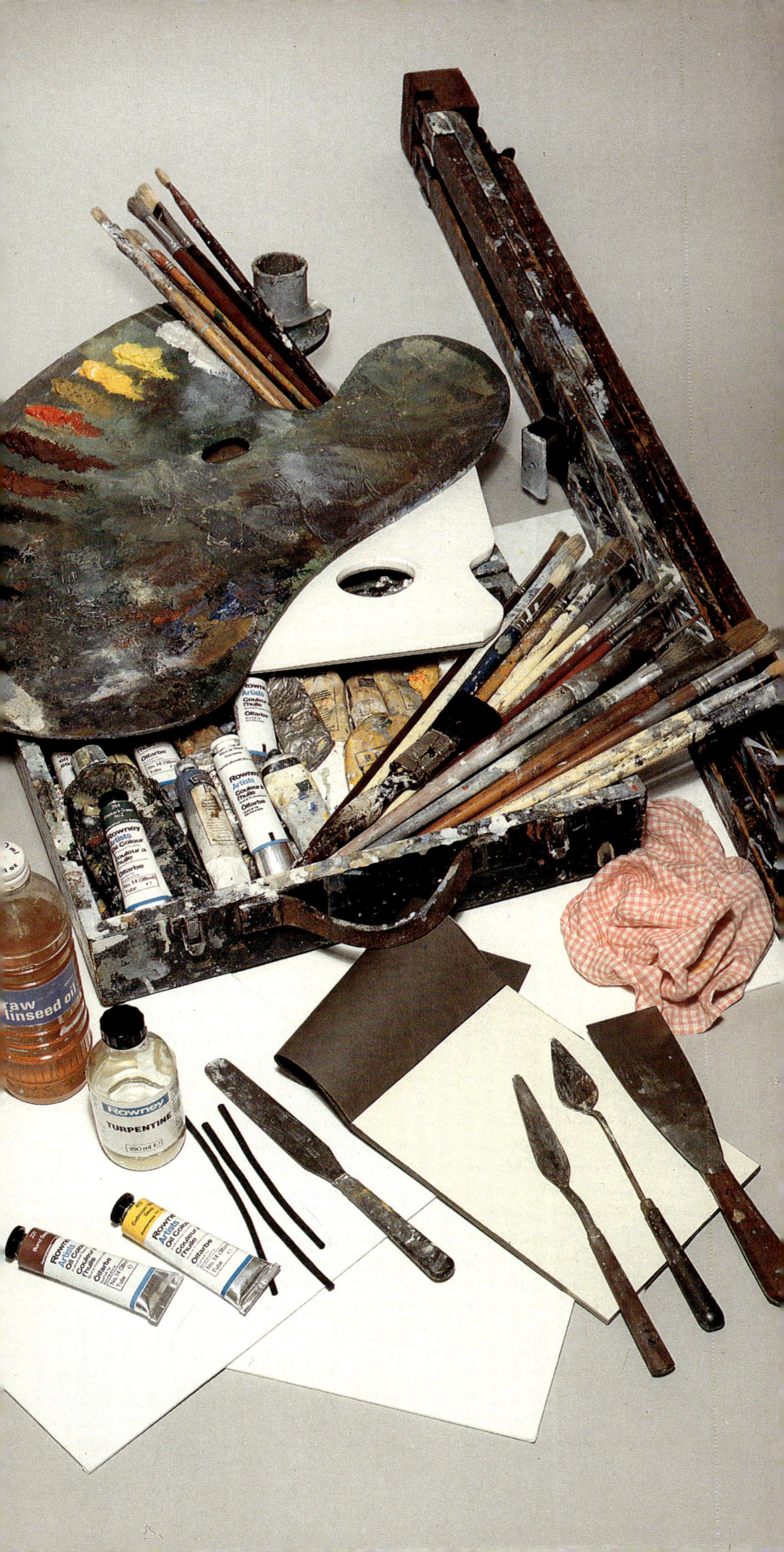

Paints

The number of different oil colours in any art shop can be staggering. It can also be baffling, because individual ranges may have similar colours under different proprietary names; and it can be off-putting, because the very fact of having so much so easily available may stop you from learning to understand the principles of colour and of colour mixing.

Working outdoors, however, can actually help you to appreciate fine pigments. Our colour codes will show you just how much can be produced from only a few basic tubes. You'll need to take with you the colours listed below.

Oil colours are pigments already mixed with a small amount of oil to help them flow. You can add more oil, or turpentine, to thin out the paint, or white to lighten the effect. Never use white spirit instead of turpentine; made of rectified paraffin, it usually contains impurities that affect some of the colours quite badly.

An important reason for mixing your own colours is that some commercially produced tones are extremely fugitive – that is, they will fade or discolour quickly. This is especially true if they are subjected to strong sunlight, as they would be out of doors.

Although there are some colours that will not be as clear in the cheaper grades, those listed below are all perfectly satisfactory in student quality. As your work improves, do add some artist's colours to your palette; they are more finely ground, have few or no additives and are of incomparable intensity.

Basic palette

White	Burnt umber
Cadmium yellow	Viridian green
Yellow ochre	Ultramarine blue
Cadmium red	Ivory black
Alizarin crimson	

Acrylic paints often have different names from traditional oil paints, and the range is much more limited. However, you will be able to find the basic seven colours you need by looking at the chart in your local supply store. If you are using canvas or boards, you will need a special acrylic primer, and there are gloss and matt mediums instead of linseed oils or turpentines. Acrylics dry more quickly than oils, are more flexible and don't harden with age or change colour, but the texture is different. Working with one or the other becomes a personal choice.

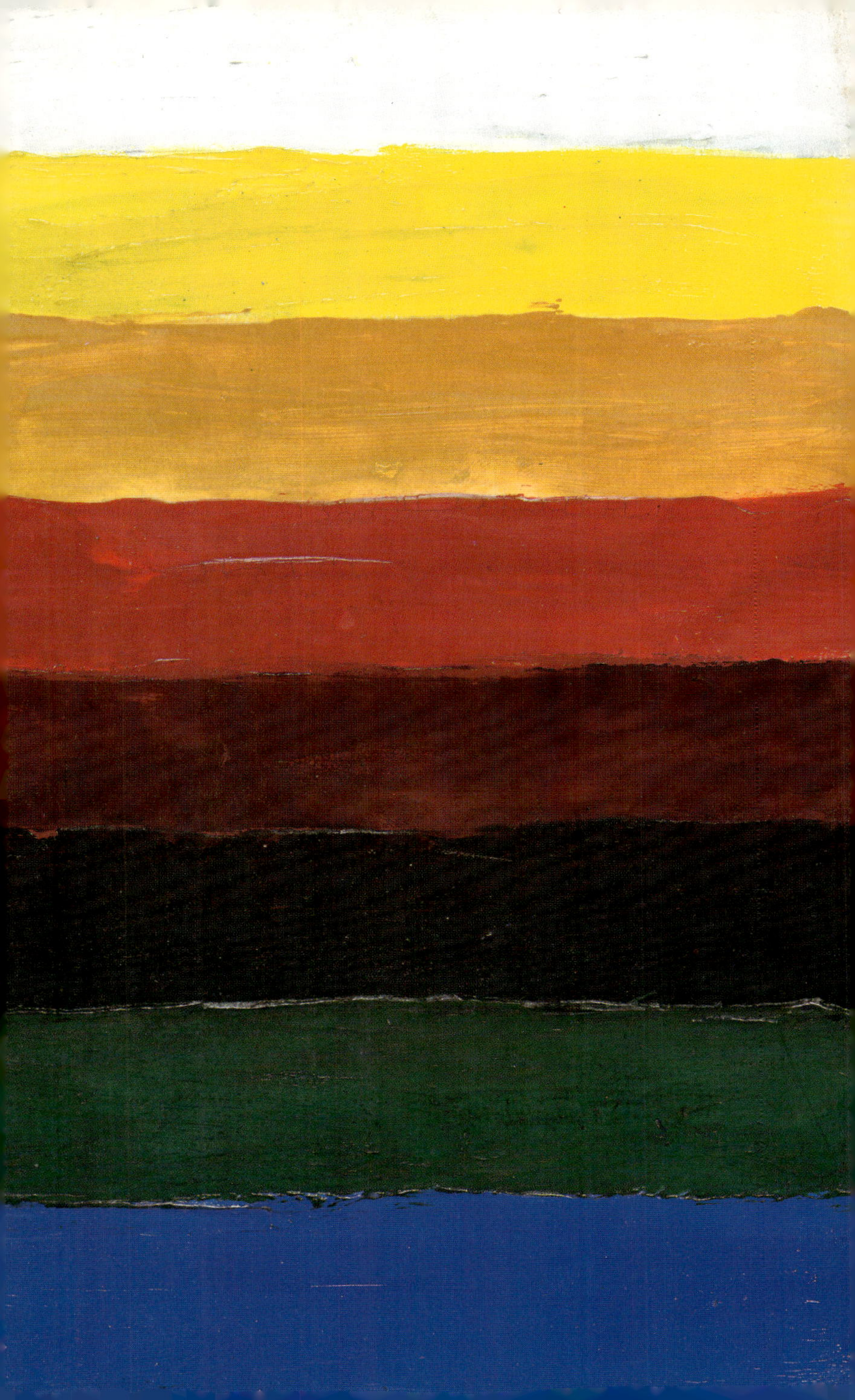

Once you have mastered the basic colours, you can add already mixed paints in a few shades to save time. The colours I would choose for any long painting trip would be those based on the earth and sky shades that I use most often in outdoor painting.

Remember that the colour will vary slightly according to how you put it onto the canvas. Like most artists I learn to work in a way that is generally known as 'lean to fat'.

In this the first washes are applied with only enough turpentine to smooth the paint into the fabric. The effect is generally quite opaque, the colours changing from the deep blobs on the palette to a much dryer, almost filmy look.

These lean washes provide the best background for any style of painting.

Gradually, as I work nearer the foreground, and therefore nearer the surface of the finished painting, I mix turpentine and/or oil with the pigment, achieving more and richer colouring, and greater depth of intensity and tone. I add the top highlights with pure pigment and oil to give a final sheen, providing sparkle and light wherever it is most appropriate.

You will find that one of the great advantages of painting in oil is that you can physically move the paint about. If you go off to lunch, leaving the painting to dry, you may well come back and decide that a section on the right or left is not what you really want; with a few flicks of the palette knife you can be back to the canvas. No other medium can be treated this way. It makes it easy to begin when you know that changing your mind is always a possibility.

Extended palette

White	Raw sienna
Lemon yellow	Burnt sienna
Cadmium yellow	Raw umber
Yellow ochre	Burnt umber
Cadmium red	Cerulean blue
Alizarin crimson	Cobalt blue
Purple	Prussian blue
Indian red	Ultramarine blue
Viridian green	Ivory black
Light green	Lamp black

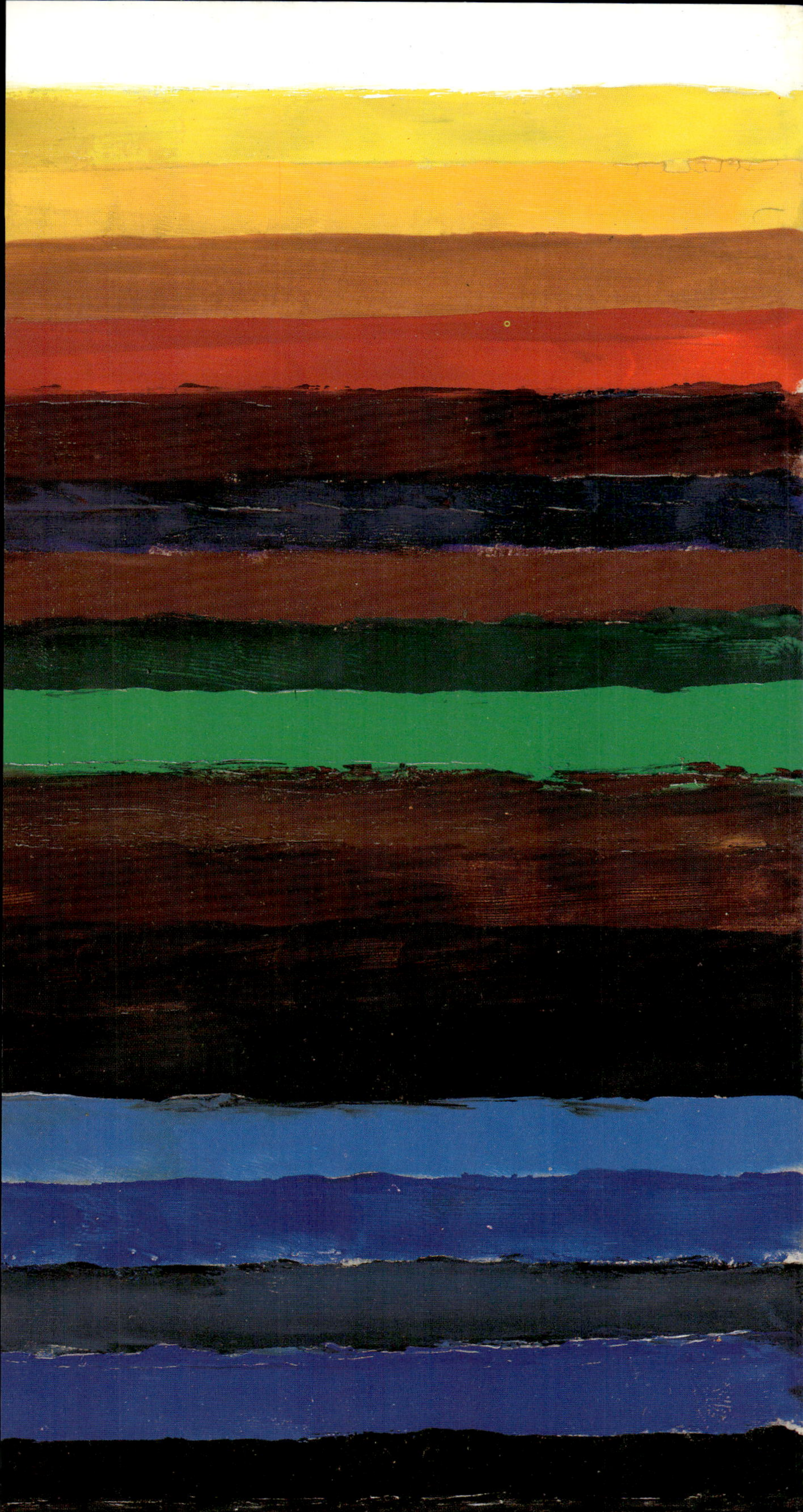

Canvas

There is almost no limit to the kinds of surface on which you can paint in oil. As with no other medium, the entire canvas is usually covered with paint, and the only part that is left showing is the weave of the fabric. Even that is becoming less true, with the growing use of ever thicker layers of pigment.

Although I prefer to carry prepared canvas boards because they are light and don't need elaborate preparation or stretching, there is a multitude of other possibilities. You can use hardboard panels, plywood or metal. All of these need to be rubbed down with sandpaper before you start work, to give the paint something to key into. This roughness is called 'tooth'.

Canvas can be bought in rolls or, more expensively, already attached to stretchers. The rule for the sort to choose is logical and easy to understand: rough for large pictures, where you will be splashing on the pigment with a certain abandon; fine-grained for small pictures, that will be worked on in thin washes and covered in fine detail.

Cotton or duck canvas is bright white, cheap and easy to stretch. Jute canvas is much stronger, darker in colour and far more expensive.

Whatever surface you choose, keep away from synthetic fabrics unless they have been especially prepared for oil painting. Otherwise, the oil may dissolve the fabric, and you could find yourself with tiny holes in your most successful picture.

Canvas boards are sold by most art shops in a wide variety of sizes. They are backed onto a kind of heavy cardboard; they are not too expensive, and provide a clean, white surface in a reasonable range of medium-rough to smooth textures. They are ideal for outdoor painters since several can be carried tied together with string. A finished board can be easily taken home, carried in your hand if necessary.

If you are using acrylics, you can also use paper; there are pads designed for use only with these paints. If you prefer to work on canvas or canvas boards, it is essential that these have been prepared for acrylics, not oils. And avoid re-using canvas that has already been painted with oils – the acrylic film will not adhere properly.

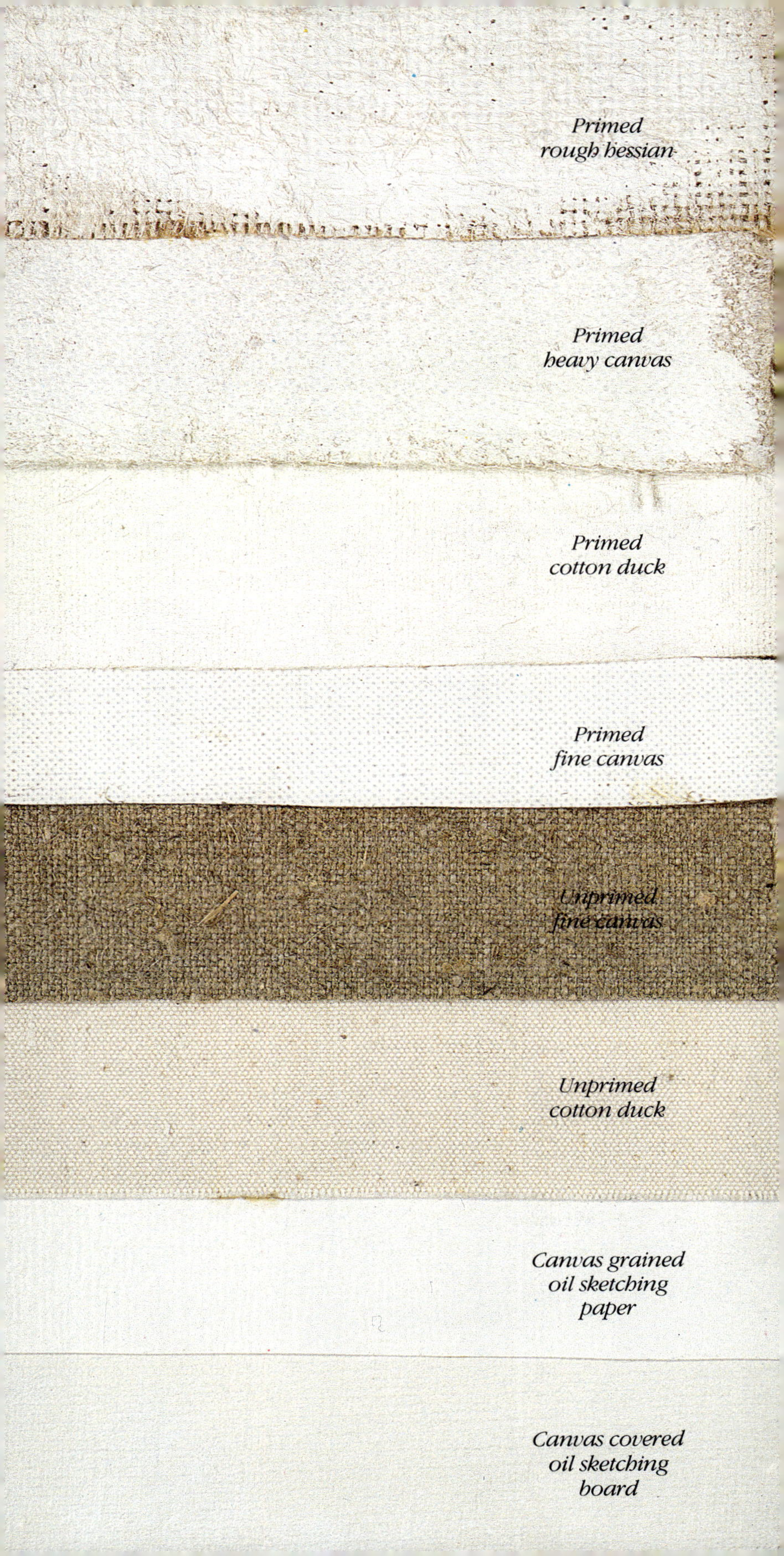

Primed
rough hessian

Primed
heavy canvas

Primed
cotton duck

Primed
fine canvas

Unprimed
fine canvas

Unprimed
cotton duck

Canvas grained
oil sketching
paper

Canvas covered
oil sketching
board

Brushes

Old-fashioned brushes were much longer, in length of hair and of handle, than their modern equivalents. Renaissance artists had brushes that they could flourish in a way that only orchestral conductors can now enjoy.

Still, for outdoor painters, it is probably less romantic but more practical to have brushes that can be held comfortably and easily, with the clipped hair which comes from short-haired animals.

Short or long, the most important points about oil brushes are having enough of them and keeping them soft and flexible.

I have dozens of brushes in my big oil-painting box, and recommend that you take at least two long-haired sable 'writers', size 4 or 6, six large hog hair brushes and six smaller hog hairs. The reason will become apparent the minute you start to work. Each brush holds one of the colours you are using, or one of the mixtures that you have made from your primary palette.

Since oil paint dries slowly, you need not dip the brush into turpentine again and again, as you do with water and watercolour; so the brush can stay either on the table or in your hand, ready to be used whenever you want to add something in that colour to the picture. This is convenient; it wastes little paint, and you don't have to clean up until the end of your day's work.

Acrylics should be washed off with water, never with turpentine, and you must not allow them to dry hard on a brush – they will be almost impossible to remove. You will have to use stainless steel or plastic palette knives.

The photograph here shows my big oil-painting palette with the colours laid out, as well as the fairly small selection of brushes that I take with me on any expedition.

I usually add another large 'house-painter's' brush, for those first wide washes of earth and sky. I keep two of these, one for the blue tones and one for the greens. Even the slightest flake of another colour on the blue brush (or vice versa) will eventually turn up just where I don't want it.

Never be afraid to spend good money on good brushes. I have had some of mine since I was twelve years old, and they are as soft and flexible as they were when I first went to art classes. Of all painter's tools, brushes become the most personal and most responsive to your way of working.

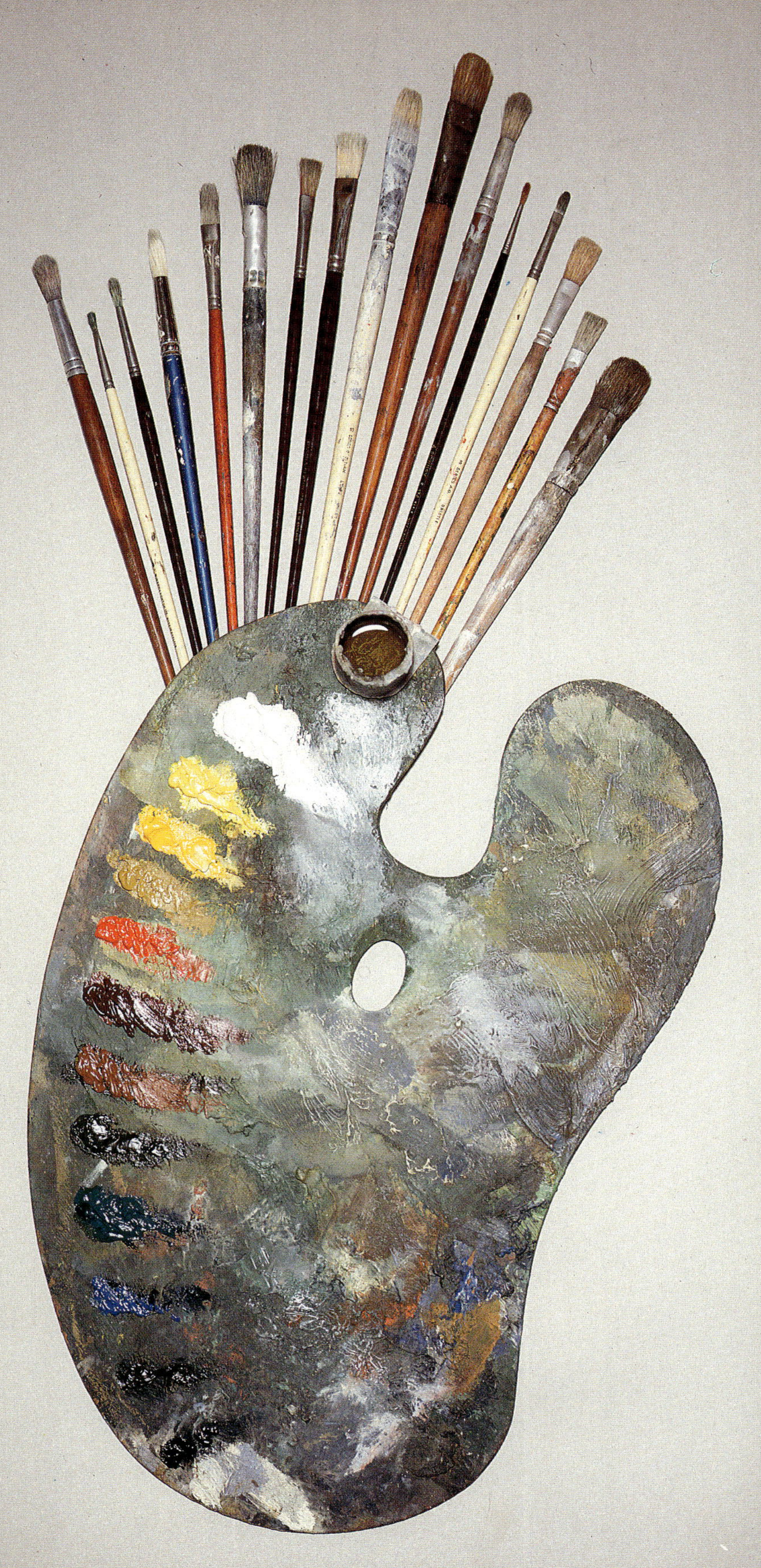

Composition

Most elements of composition are common to all painting, but there are some special factors that need to be considered in oil painting. A good composition is pleasing to the eye, and has carefully structured tone, colour and perspective.

One of the problems with oil is that the very intensity of the colours may make it difficult to appreciate the perspective and tone patterns that would be obvious in a drawing or a watercolour. That is one reason why many painters begin with line and tone sketches before they start an oil painting.

However, I would suggest that you try to work out the composition directly on the canvas. This gives you practice in learning to see for yourself, and in transferring what you see from the real landscape to your picture.

Use the viewing frame to select a view that you think will make a pleasant composition. Choose a shape that is similar to the shape of your canvas – square, horizontal, or rectangular.

Look carefully at the view, and try to isolate in your mind the first two masses: the sky and the earth.

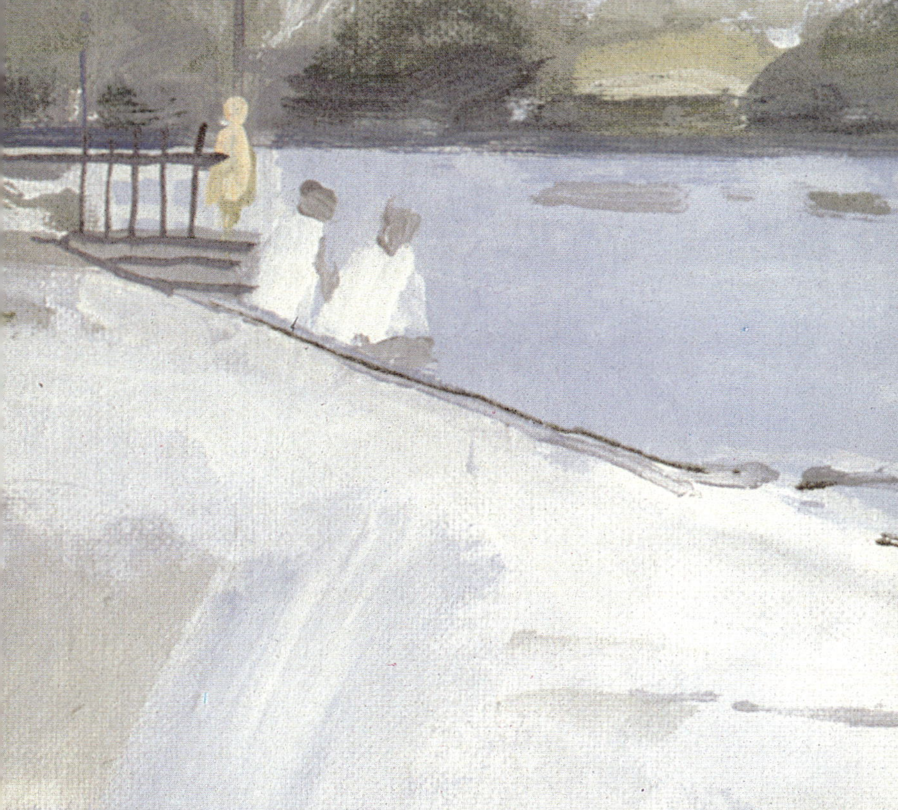

Next, look at the tones. Where are the dark, the medium and the light of any form or pattern? This is where colour can be distracting. A light colour is not necessarily a bright colour, and its position in the picture will also change its tone.

Don't assume that objects that are at different distances from you are the same tone – or even the same colour. In general, anything in the foreground will be deeper in tone, and stronger in colour. As it moves into the background the tone becomes lighter and the colour lighter, too.

A black car in the foreground will be very black indeed, but at the end of a road it may look pale grey. When you paint trees, those in the foreground may be a strong, warm green with dark blue-green shadows. The same trees in the distance can be pale blue-green, with light grey shadows.

Compare different parts of your picture to make sure that changes in colour and tone are accurately recorded.

It is important to remember that dark colours can be as mixed in tone as bright colours. Purples are full of rich shadows, and blacks are seldom solid areas of flat black.

Scale is a vital part of your composition. Without something for the eye to recognize – and with which to compare – it is often difficult to tell whether a small rise is a hill or a towering mountain, whether a patch of blue is a puddle or a lake.

This is particularly true with oils, where a broad brush stroke may just as easily be a foreground bush as a distant tree.

Figures are useful to help the viewer's eye adjust to the scale of the picture, but you can also use buildings, whose window and door frames provide natural reference points for scale. Remember that you need not reject a composition because it lacks such objects.

You can add figures or buildings – or indeed anything you choose – just as you can move trees or fields to help make a better picture.

Using sharp angles as I have done here is an excellent way to divide the canvas, making different shapes that can be manipulated to provide more excitement and interest than a horizontal line would have done. When you experiment in this way, you will achieve different results that you can compare, and from which you learn, thus developing an analytical way to look at landscape.

Choosing a view

Townscapes

Painting outdoor urban scenes in oils creates a great many problems for artists. For a start, there is the need to find somewhere to sit comfortably, with enough space to put out your equipment, where you can stay long enough to accomplish something without getting into people's way.

Unused doorways are an obvious choice, but they must be fairly deep so that your easel doesn't stick out and force pedestrians to walk around you.

Park benches are ideal. They are made to be sat on; they often face a pleasant view, and there is usually enough space to set up without obstructing other people.

The next problem is the light. Tall buildings and busy streets produce strange shadow patterns which can change dramatically as the sky darkens towards evening, or with an approaching storm.

Go back to the principle of deciding what you want to paint – a sunny day or a cloudy day, for example. Then keep to that palette, even if the real sky changes. If you are unable to retain a particular colour or a specially shadowed place in your memory, stop painting and return on another day when the conditions are similar to those of your first experience.

You might find it useful to make colour swatches of the sky and of important buildings or roof lines before you actually start on your big picture. That way, no matter what happens later, you will have a physical record of the colours you began with.

Another problem is movement. People are seldom in less than a hurry; buses and cars roar by, and it might seem impossible to record anything at all in only a few seconds of comparative quiet.

Here the answer is to select exactly what you want. Look carefully at the things you would like to include and freeze them in your mind. Then paint what you see in your memory rather than what is passing in front of you.

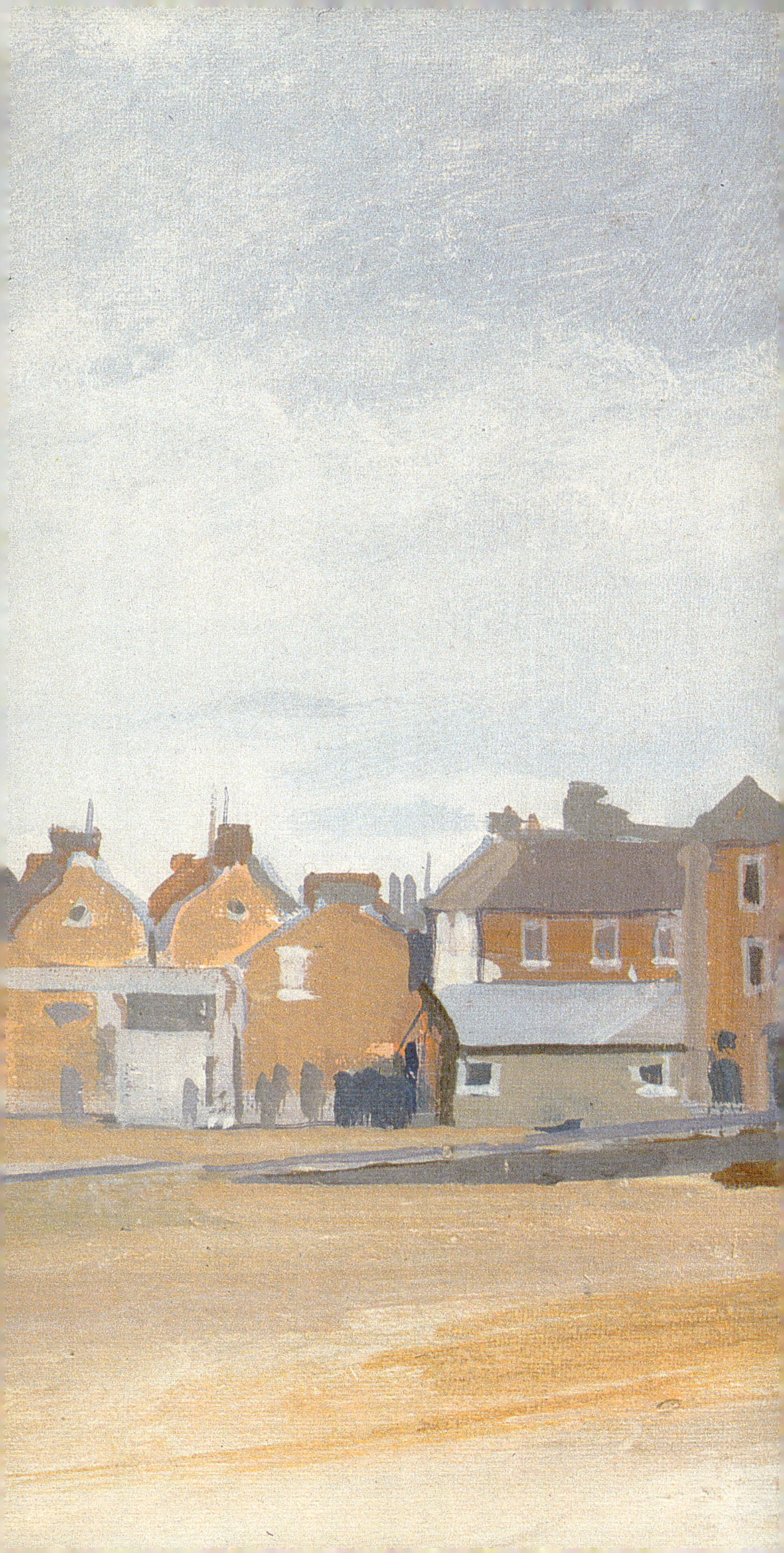

Countryside

In many ways, the countryside is a paradise for oil painters: plenty of space; plenty of light and air; shelter usually available, and few troublesome changing patterns of people or traffic.

Yet there is one problem that is seldom recognized but is probably responsible for more bad countryside pictures than any other single factor: the horizon – or lack of it. If you have a long view from your easel, all is solved. There is your distance, then your middle distance, then your foreground.

However, the country is full of pleasant paintable scenes that have no horizons. A village green, backed by a wood, might look perfect as you drive past – until you realize that there is nothing to give you depth and space. Everything is right in front of you. The trees rise up and hide the line where the sky deepens towards the earth. You will have to manufacture your own feeling of recession in order to give your painting the necessary solidity. Overhanging trees provide more of the same – too many greens, too much alike and without depth or contrast of light. You will end up with a rather boring composition. So look for something to break the line – a church spire, a farm building, even a telegraph pole.

Try to see the skeleton of the tree inside the leaves. This is easy in winter and early spring, harder in the lush growth of full summer. But use your artistic licence and make the branches and the colour of the bark a little more prominent than in the real thing.

The country is also the place to remember your good manners. Somehow, being almost entirely alone on a grass verge or by a farm entrance makes some artists forget that they are responsible for litter and for carelessness. Leaving gates open is unforgivable even if the field looks totally unoccupied; animals may be moved into the area from another entrance.

Tubes of paint left lying about are poisonous to many living creatures; some pigments are still made with dangerous compounds and dyes.

And I have actually seen students wipe their palette knives or brushes on gateposts as well as on convenient bushes. Then the farmer (or indeed, the next painter!) comes along, reaches for the gate and is left with a handful of deep Cobalt blue or Viridian green.

Remember oil paint may take days or even weeks to dry. Being an artist is not a licence to disregard being a good neighbour.

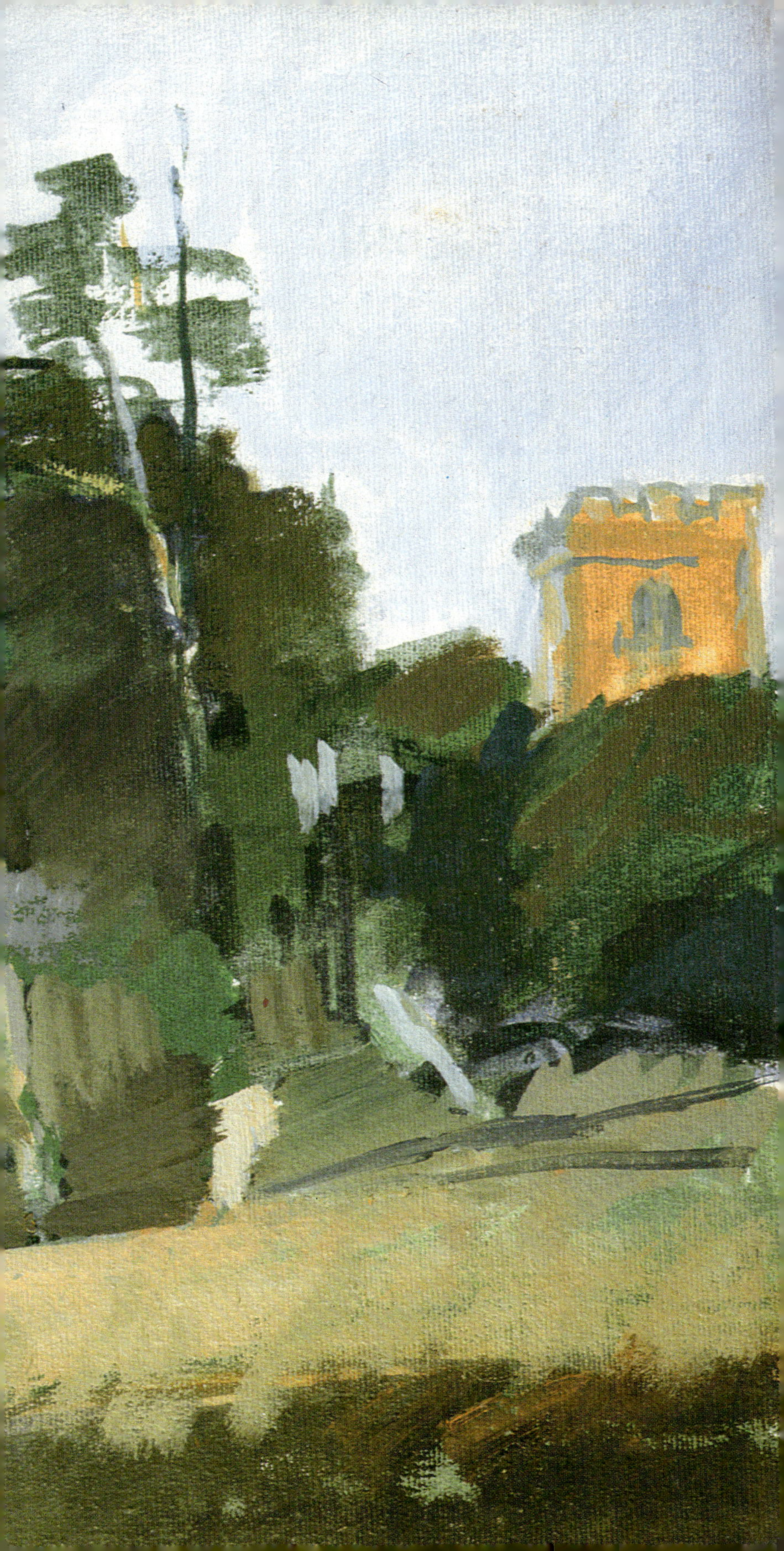

If all else fails ...

When the paint box seems too heavy, when you've hurt your ankle or sprained your knee, or when you simply haven't the time to go more than a few yards away from home, there is still a great deal you can do.

You could, of course, work on a small section of a tree, or a stone wall, or a brick, but that kind of close-up does not often seem appropriate to the thick texture and rough brush strokes of oil paints.

So find something that will occur again and again in any landscape – a patch of grass in the foreground. For your purposes, it can be a patch on your lawn – near a garden path, full of weeds or as smooth as a bowling green.

Get down as near to eye level as possible, so that you see the textures and tones of the grass from the side. Think of yourself as a small animal and see the patch as an overwhelming landscape instead of the few small blades and top colouring it would be from normal head height.

The idea is to observe and record how the stems and flowering tops cross each other, forming their own natural patterns. You should also look for changes in the texture of the grasses: some will be very thin and transparent, some thick and woody. Some will grow into narrow points, some into spray heads similar to wheat, and some will burst out into tiny flowerheads.

Think about putting as much of this variety as possible into your picture, even though you are using light strokes of colour.

Look at the colours carefully, too. There will be many different greens in one very small area, and near the ground the colour will seem very much stronger than near the top where the grass is touched by sunlight.

After making your first sketches, try to record another sketch with the emphasis on the patterns of growth. Grass left to grow naturally in the middle of the lawn has a natural rhythm which is missing where the seeds have been pushed aside by the edges of the path.

By building up a series of different sketches, each of which picks out the details which characterise the various patterns you encounter, you will sharpen your powers of observation.

This kind of minute observation can be used for the foreground of many oil paintings, not only with grass but with, for instance, a puddle, a stretch of gravel driveway, a stony path or the bottom of a hedge.

Try all of these on a small oil sketching pad. Pin up the results around your work room and let the impact gradually sink in as you learn to assess what you have done and to discover what particular details you need to try again.

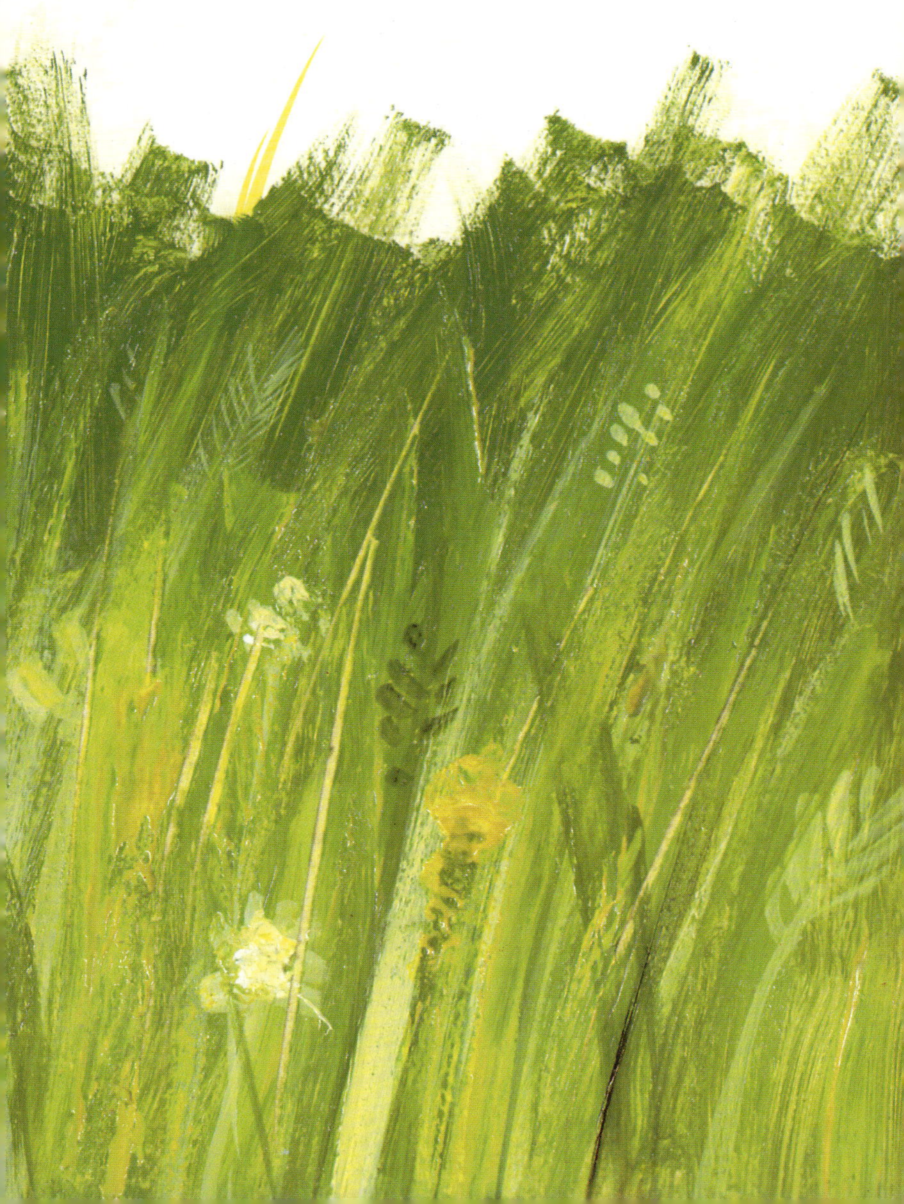

Special notes

People

Figures in a landscape appear throughout classical painting, and are often added deliberately even when there is no one in sight in order to give scale and a sense of proportion to the view.

Sometimes, of course, the figure is an important part of the painting – a farmer or a woman sitting on a chair inside a doorway, for example – and must be treated like any portrait. Begin by sketching the figure in your notebook, just to make sure you have the proportions and position right, then transfer that image in your mind to the canvas in front of you.

Don't try to do a painting with an important figure in it unless you are sure the person will be there for a least half an hour, or unless you can make so many different sketches that you will be able to reproduce the figure from your notebook and your memory.

However, most outdoor paintings are land- or cityscapes in which the figures are moving rather than static. Try to capture them with a minimum of brush strokes. Sketch the basic bulk in first, then add a few short strokes for boots, the heads and the bags or parcels which are part of the scene. This will give the feeling of spontaneity and movement that is so important to the atmosphere of your finished work.

Look carefully at what the figures are doing and depict their tools and equipment as realistically as you can. Make sure that the sack of coal is solid and heavy, that the rake is being used amidst a few wispy strands of hay. This is the key to making the figures real.

Other kinds of people-orientated sketches are also good to do in oil. Try a 'time lapse' series of small oil sketches.

Find a comfortable seat near a market or busy farmyard. Then do a number of quick paintings as people come and go. Try one in the early morning, working through until lunchtime. Then start a new picture showing all the lunchtime bustle. As the busy scene fades into mid-afternoon, you'll have the subject of another painting, with different lighting conditions.

Work on a small scale so that you can finish within an hour or two – but not so small that you have nothing at all in your picture.

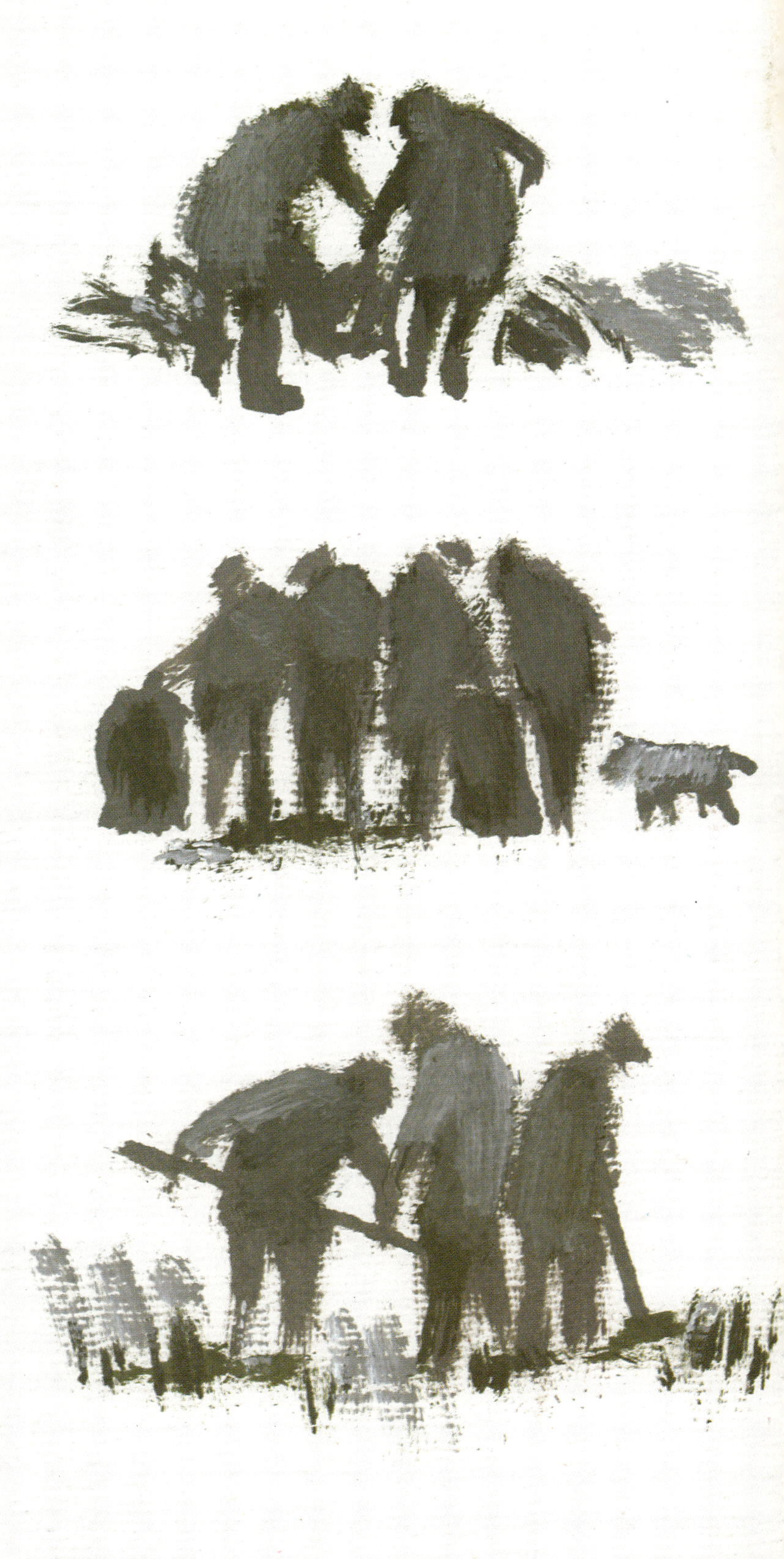

Buildings

One of the problems in oil painting is that architectural details
are so fine that many artists find it almost impossible to
reproduce them with brush and thick pigment, rather than fine
pencil or the very narrow brushes used in watercolour painting.

However, this can be overcome by first simplifying the outline
of the detail, then working out *from* this outline *to* the building
as a whole.

I usually paint the background colour of the building first, as a
mass rather than as a filled-in block of colour. The edges can be
very fuzzy, and far from exact. If I'm painting a window, I then
look at the shape of the glass area. This is physically behind the
frame, but it is also the darkest of the colours. I paint the whole
glass area, then add the outline of the frame, and finally a band
of colour to indicate the lintel and arch or architrave. This will
vary, because of the different colours that are used and also
because the shadow may be slightly different depending where
on the facade a window is.

I then add the other windows, making sure they are correctly
positioned in relation to the first. The line of the sills should
recede naturally if you are looking at the windows from the side,
even though the shadows and the surroundings may change the
overall shape.

Try to simplify all the time. You are not attempting to make an
architectural drawing, even though you want to convey the
flavour of the building, the impression it gives and the balance
it adds to the street or its setting.

Making quick sketches like these window progressions is much
easier and quicker when you use acrylics, and this is perhaps the
most appropriate advantage of all the various acrylic mixtures.
You can paint the glass first and then, within a very short time,
paint the divisions and glazing bars right over the top. Do
remember that colours change as they recede – see how the
black glass has become grey in the first series.

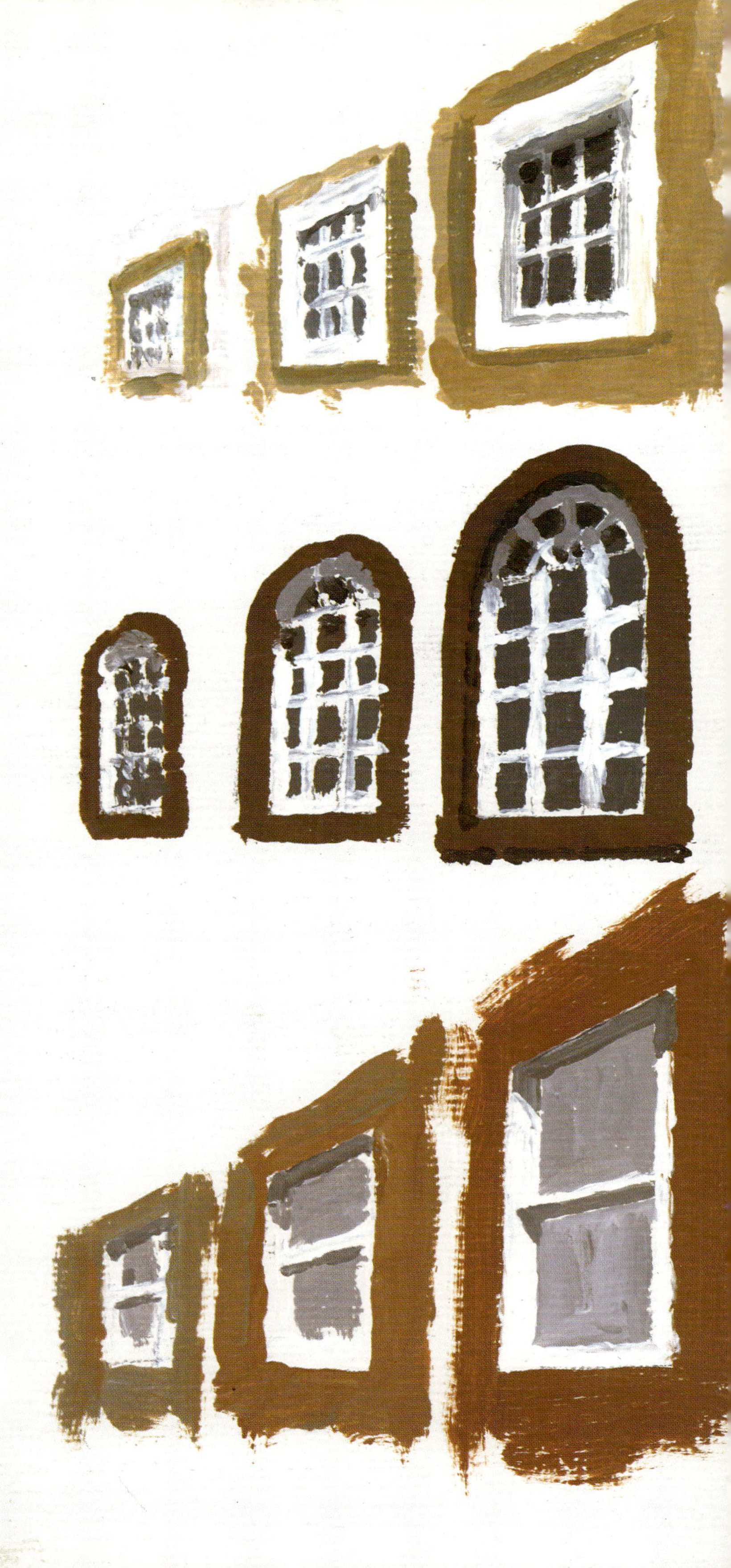

Waterscapes

Water, endlessly fascinating, provides some of the most picturesque scenes any artist could imagine. In one setting you may find glitter and depth, colour and sweeps of texture, translucency, reflections and double images.

If you add the drama of sandy beaches, rocky cliffs, harbours and marinas, boats and sailing ships, you can understand why some painters build their studios on the water's edge, never to move again.

When I decide to work on a waterscape, the first consideration is the general atmosphere of the place I am looking at. At the seaside the colour of the water can be misleading. Near tropical islands, it may be brilliant turquoise, but in the northern hemisphere the blue of the sea is almost always blue-grey and silver, and it will reflect the sky, the sunset or the darkness of an approaching storm.

There is nothing tangible in the scene – few subjects, even fewer objects – and there may be a sense of unease caused by the continual movement of everything in view. The sea and the sky are in constant motion, and staring too long could even make you seasick!

Doing such a scene, I use a series of washes almost like watercolours, working straight across the canvas with gentle gradations of colour towards the horizon where the two grey-blues meet. The sense of movement in the water can be emphasized by tiny flecks of colour and pure white.

A river is quite a different matter. Here there are reflections and often great stillness. You may be painting two landscapes at once, the scene above the river bank, and its mirror image below. Using the same colours, you should paint both together, defining the reflections by the texture of your brush marks rather than by harsh changes in colour.

The intention should be to create a flowing scene that matches the mood of the river, your brush flowing with the tide as if it were a kind of calligraphy.

A beach scene is different still. Here you can have fun with the interaction among three elements instead of two: the sea, the beach, the sky. With the addition of my favourite boats, a few deck-chairs and a pier or a marina a lively composition develops easily.

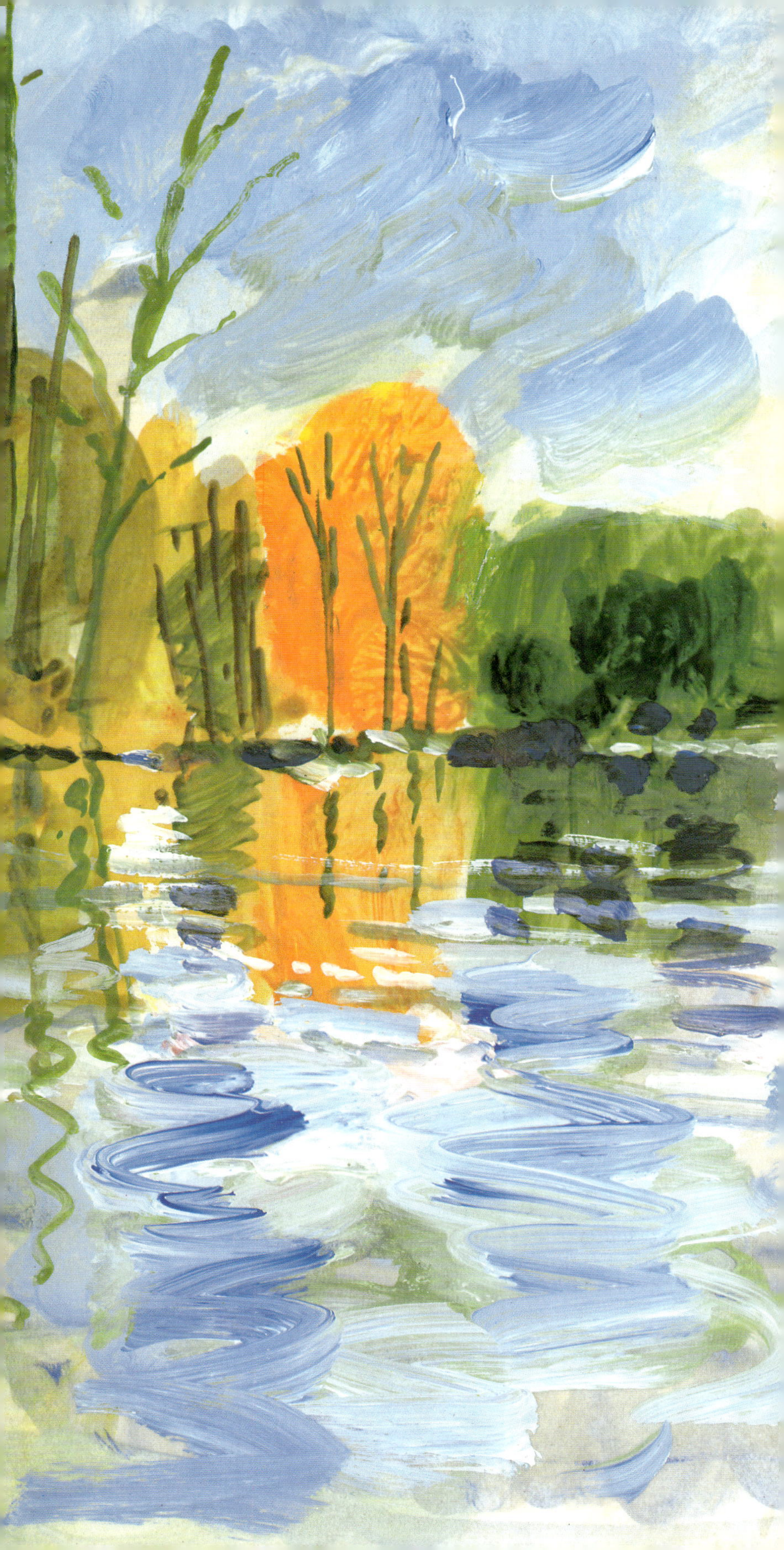

Texture

As this detail shows, oil paint can be built up to have a real
profile, and impasto – thickly laying on colour – is a kind of low
relief that can be used to shape and control both colour and
form.

Although most people think that heavy paint is always put on
with a palette knife, this is not so. A brush is perfectly capable of
creating thick strokes, full of rich track lines made when the
hairs are dragged across the surface. I believe that these marks
are much more interesting than the flat chunky surfaces left by
the knife.

The important point to remember when you work in impasto is
that you must use the paint as the object, not as an outline
around it. If you lay a flower petal over the background in a
brilliant vivid red, that brush stroke *is* the petal. If you shape a
stand of trees, as I did here on the banks of the Thames, those
strokes become the trees.

Should you try to use impasto to work around an object, the
relief effect disappears; the object will recede into the painting
and leave you with a strange and almost meaningless shape
around an empty-looking space.

Once you have begun to master impasto, you may enjoy the
effect so much that you will want to work on an entire painting
in the same low relief. Remember to follow the golden rule of
distance: even with layers and layers of paint, the furthest objects
should always be painted first.

Remember, too, that on the whole impasto is never as detailed
nor as precise as a flat wash painting, so you will have to stand
back quite a way in order to judge whether you are getting the
right effect. You will also have to learn to paint from further away
in order to keep your eye in touch with what your hand is doing.

Finally, although you can use impasto in the foreground for
almost any painting, the reverse is not true. A flat-wash
foreground would look extremely odd with a heavy impasto sky,
for example.

This is quite logical in that it follows the experiences and
capabilities of the human eye. Whatever you see immediately in
front of you may be quite coarse and grainy, even if the
background recedes gradually into a haze of flat colour.

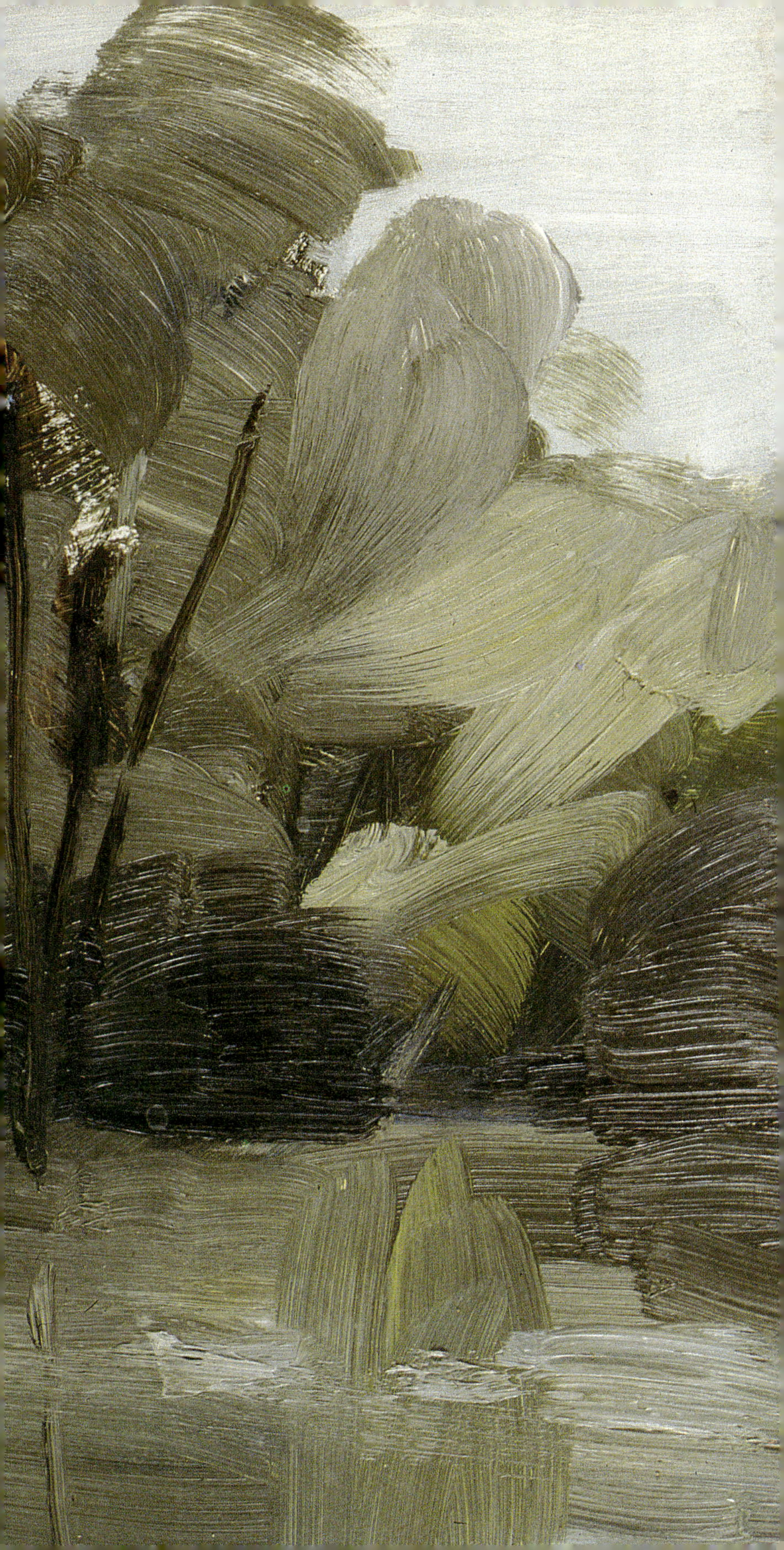

Skies

As a general rule, outdoor oil painters work from the
background to the foreground. This is partly because the paint
itself has such covering possibilities that you need to put the
nearest things 'on top' to make them look right. As far as the sky
is concerned, I believe that if you put any colour under the final
pale blue, it will somehow change or distort it.

There is a logical progression to this, too. If you begin with the
most distant area, usually the sky, the clouds painted on top will
look as they do in nature – as if they were moving across the
background. If you paint the clouds first, and then work the sky
around them, you will have pale blue circles and wave marks
around white patches, which will look very strange.

So begin by laying your wash of blue across the area you plan to
allot to the sky. And that brings you to your next problem – the
horizon. Look at a Constable or a Turner landscape and you will
see that the sky is never completely separate from the land; the
two blend subtly together, the line often broken up with trees
or spires. As the sky comes near to the earth, it picks up some of
the earthy colours, as it would pick up the cold grey of the sea
in a marine painting. Your second wash will be over the land
area in the painting, leaving a fairly blurred line where sky and
land meet. From then on, you should work gradually forward,
adding trees, buildings, people and so on as they come nearer.

Once you have painted in the sky, you can add clouds whenever
you like, remembering to watch the light reflections from the
earth as well as the contrast with the sky colours. If the sky is so
full of cloud that scarcely any blue shows, it may be sensible to
lay a wash of pale grey rather than blue, adding billows or
movement on top. This is the one time when you can add a few
blue patches without its looking unnatural.

When you paint in the city, especially at dusk or at night, the sky
will hold reflections from street lights, shop signs and so on.
These are easier to discern near the horizon than overhead.

Few painters try to re-create a night sky in the country unless
there is a great deal of moonlight; even then it is difficult, for you
are still painting in the dark!

Early morning and evening skies are perhaps the most beautiful
of all, full of shifting colours, warm lights and drifting clouds.
These are magic to look at and even more magical to paint. Plan
some painting trips at these hours, to discover how much beauty
of a new kind you can bring home.

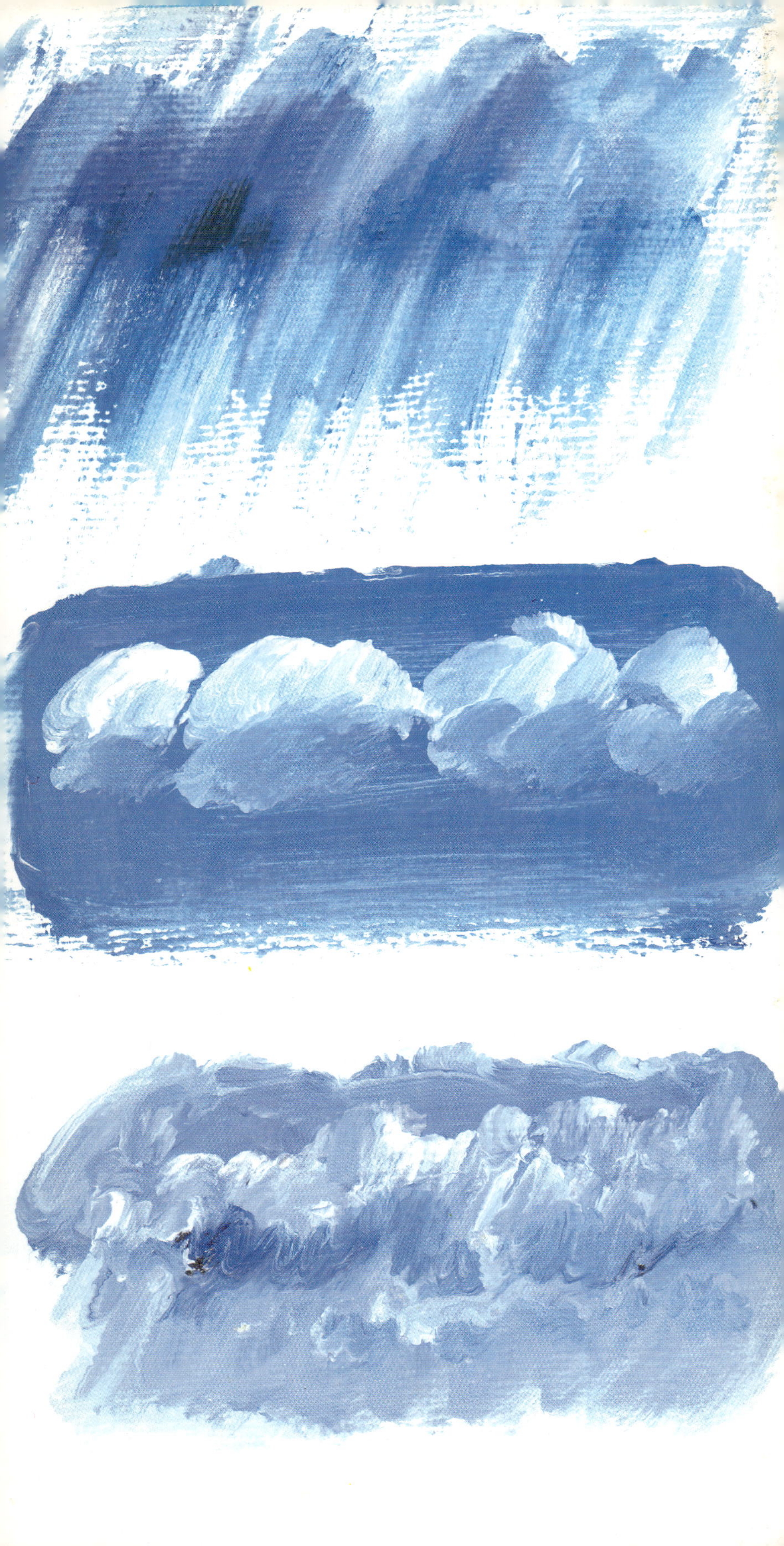

Colour codes

Painting outdoors always makes a big difference to how you see and understand colours and their relationships to each other. The light coming from all directions saturates the canvas and your palette in a way that is unknown in a studio working area.

This is why painting at home or indoors never gives an accurate estimate of what you need to reproduce the particular blue of the sky, or the special yellow-green of mustard fields in the distance. The colour codes have been developed to help you in three ways, depending on how and what you are doing.

If you are simply enjoying an afternoon of recreation, the blocks of colour and their proportions will help you find exactly the tone you want as quickly as possible.

Hold up the book so that you see the charts at eye level, looking beyond to the natural colour in the landscape. Don't try to find the right tone with the book lying flat in front of you. Changes in the way the light hits the page will give a false impression.

If you are seriously interested in colour, the progression through some of the basic palette colours will provide a good education in how pigments change and react with each other. Each code has its own logic and each is an important step in the artist's vocabulary of colour relationships.

Unlike watercolour, oil pigments are opaque and can be mixed to give a very even, almost flat single colour. I have chosen to do a series of progressions with the three basic yellows because the change in each case is quite subtle; and with yellow and a variety of greens and blues you achieve most of the most commonly used landscape colours.

The final colour code gives different values, mixing earth yellows with reds and browns.

However, the section begins with two very straightforward charts. The first, on the opposite page, shows how oil colours can be manipulated in four ways. The orange band is taken, with turpentine, through darker tones to red. The second band starts with green and mutates into purple. The third and fourth bands are mixed with white to give in each case the lighter and lightest tones of green and black.

On the following page, there is a more complete look at how white can completely alter the weight and intensity of the basic colours.

It is a good idea for more advanced painters to make up individual colour charts with the colours they think are particularly pleasing, and which they will be using most often.

The most commonly used colours in oil pigments are shown opposite, progressively lightened by white.

White is used much more extensively in oil than in watercolour. This is because the canvas does not work as a white surface in the same way that paper does; the pigments are usually too dense and too opaque for that. Oil painters therefore use considerable quantities of Titanium or Zinc white (not Flake, which is a lead-based paint, and highly toxic) and it is important to understand how this changes both the tone and the intensity of colour. Modern painters mix the pigment on the canvas instead of on the palette. This can give additional texture to the area as the colours are striated, showing brush marks, rather than completely blended.

Whenever you buy a new colour, or even a different brand of the same colour, try it out in various configurations. Blend it with turpentine, with oil and with white, in a series of bands similar to the pattern on the opposite page. Add additional colours to the next bands, contrasting and blending until you begin to appreciate the many variations you will be able to achieve with just one new tube.

Colours blended with white:

Cadmium yellow
Yellow ochre
Cadmium red
Alizarin crimson
Burnt umber
Viridian green
Prussian blue
Ultramarine blue

If you are trying out acrylic colours, you will be mixing them with the appropriate medium instead of oil or turpentine. Acrylic gloss medium keeps the colours translucent and shiny, and there is usually a gel which will thicken the paint for heavier textures. All the colours can be mixed with white in the usual way, or diluted with a flow improver which makes the pigment more liquid without diluting the strength of the colour.

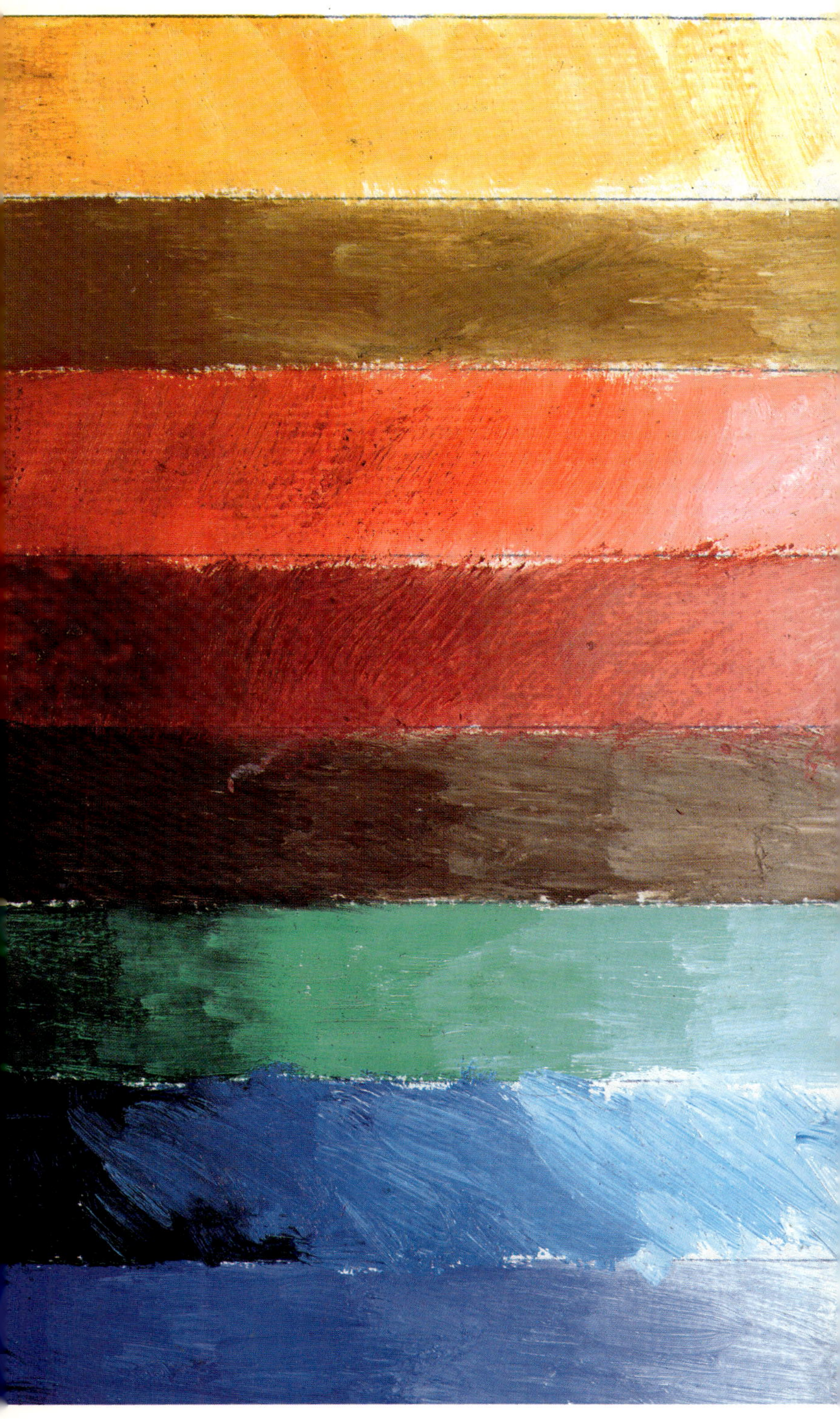

Lemon yellow	Lemon yellow 3 Viridian green 1	Lemon yellow 2 Viridian green 2	Lemon yellow 1 Viridian green 3	Viridian green
Lemon yellow	Lemon yellow 3 Olive green 1	Lemon yellow 2 Olive green 2	Lemon yellow 1 Olive green 3	Olive green
Lemon yellow	Lemon yellow 3 Sap green 1	Lemon yellow 2 Sap green 2	Lemon yellow 1 Sap green 3	Sap green
Lemon yellow	Lemon yellow 3 Cerulean blue 1	Lemon yellow 2 Cerulean blue 2	Lemon yellow 1 Cerulean blue 3	Cerulean blue
Lemon yellow	Lemon yellow 3 Cobalt blue 1	Lemon yellow 2 Cobalt blue 2	Lemon yellow 1 Cobalt blue 3	Cobalt blue
Lemon yellow	Lemon yellow 3 Ultramarine blue 1	Lemon yellow 2 Ultramarine blue 2	Lemon yellow 1 Ultramarine blue 3	Ultramarine blue
Lemon yellow	Lemon yellow 3 Prussian blue 1	Lemon yellow 2 Prussian blue 2	Lemon yellow 1 Prussian blue 3	Prussian blue
Lemon yellow	Lemon yellow 3 Black 1	Lemon yellow 2 Black 2	Lemon yellow 1 Black 3	Black

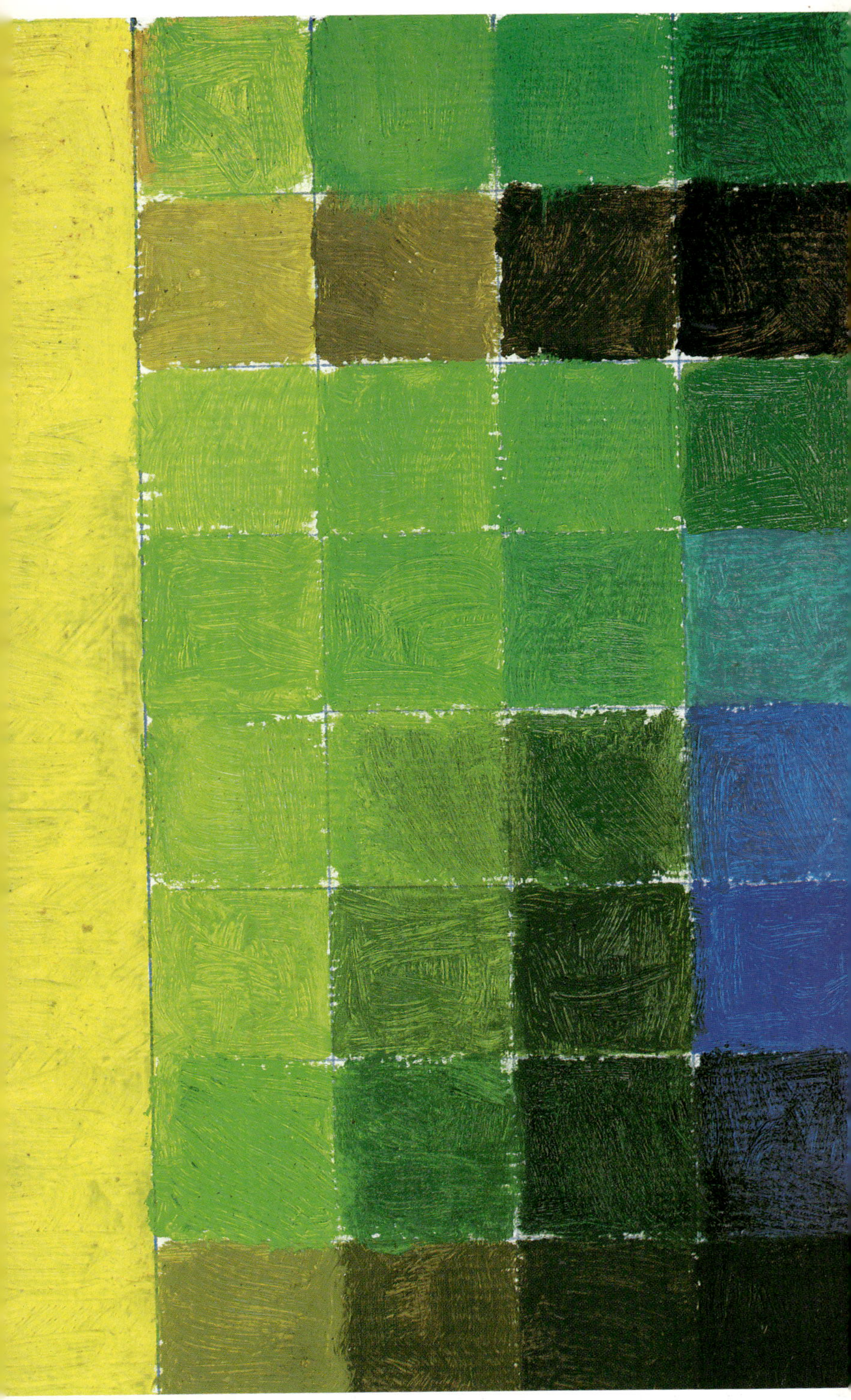

Cadmium yellow	Cadmium yellow 3 Viridian green 1	Cadmium yellow 2 Viridian green 2	Cadmium yellow 1 Viridian green 3	Viridian green
Cadmium yellow	Cadmium yellow 3 Olive green 1	Cadmium yellow 2 Olive green 2	Cadmium yellow 1 Olive green 3	Olive green
Cadmium yellow	Cadmium yellow 3 Sap green 1	Cadmium yellow 2 Sap green 2	Cadmium yellow 1 Sap green 3	Sap green
Cadmium yellow	Cadmium yellow 3 Cerulean blue 1	Cadmium yellow 2 Cerulean blue 2	Cadmium yellow 1 Cerulean blue 3	Cerulean blue
Cadmium yellow	Cadmium yellow 3 Cobalt blue 1	Cadmium yellow 2 Cobalt blue 2	Cadmium yellow 1 Cobalt blue 3	Cobalt blue
Cadmium yellow	Cadmium yellow 3 Ultramarine blue 1	Cadmium yellow 2 Ultramarine blue 2	Cadmium yellow 1 Ultramarine blue 3	Ultramarine blue
Cadmium yellow	Cadmium yellow 3 Prussian blue 1	Cadmium yellow 2 Prussian blue 2	Cadmium yellow 1 Prussian blue 3	Prussian blue
Cadmium yellow	Cadmium yellow 3 Black 1	Cadmium yellow 2 Black 2	Cadmium yellow 1 Black 3	Black

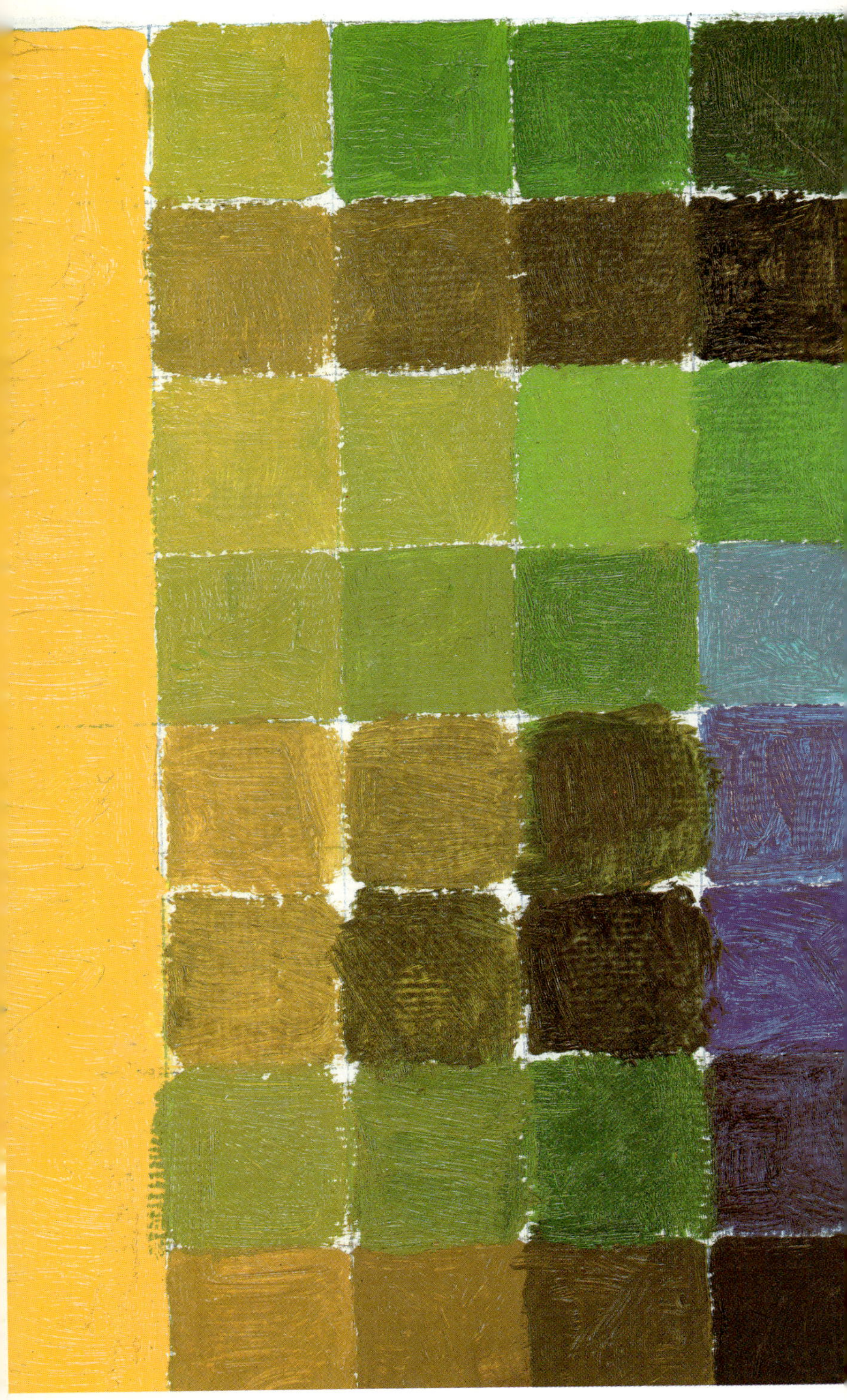

Cadmium orange	Cadmium orange 3 Viridian green 1	Cadmium orange 2 Viridian green 2	Cadmium orange 1 Viridian green 3	Viridian green
Cadmium orange	Cadmium orange 3 Olive green 1	Cadmium orange 2 Olive green 2	Cadmium orange 1 Olive green 3	Olive green
Cadmium orange	Cadmium orange 3 Sap green 1	Cadmium orange 2 Sap green 2	Cadmium orange 1 Sap green 3	Sap green
Cadmium orange	Cadmium orange 3 Cerulean blue 1	Cadmium orange 2 Cerulean blue 2	Cadmium orange 1 Cerulean blue 3	Cerulean blue
Cadmium orange	Cadmium orange 3 Cobalt blue 1	Cadmium orange 2 Cobalt blue 2	Cadmium orange 1 Cobalt blue 3	Cobalt blue
Cadmium orange	Cadmium orange 3 Ultramarine blue 1	Cadmium orange 2 Ultramarine blue 2	Cadmium orange 1 Ultramarine blue 3	Ultramarine blue
Cadmium orange	Cadmium orange 3 Prussian blue 1	Cadmium orange 2 Prussian blue 2	Cadmium orange 1 Prussian blue 3	Prussian blue
Cadmium orange	Cadmium orange 3 Black 1	Cadmium orange 2 Black 2	Cadmium orange 1 Black 3	Black

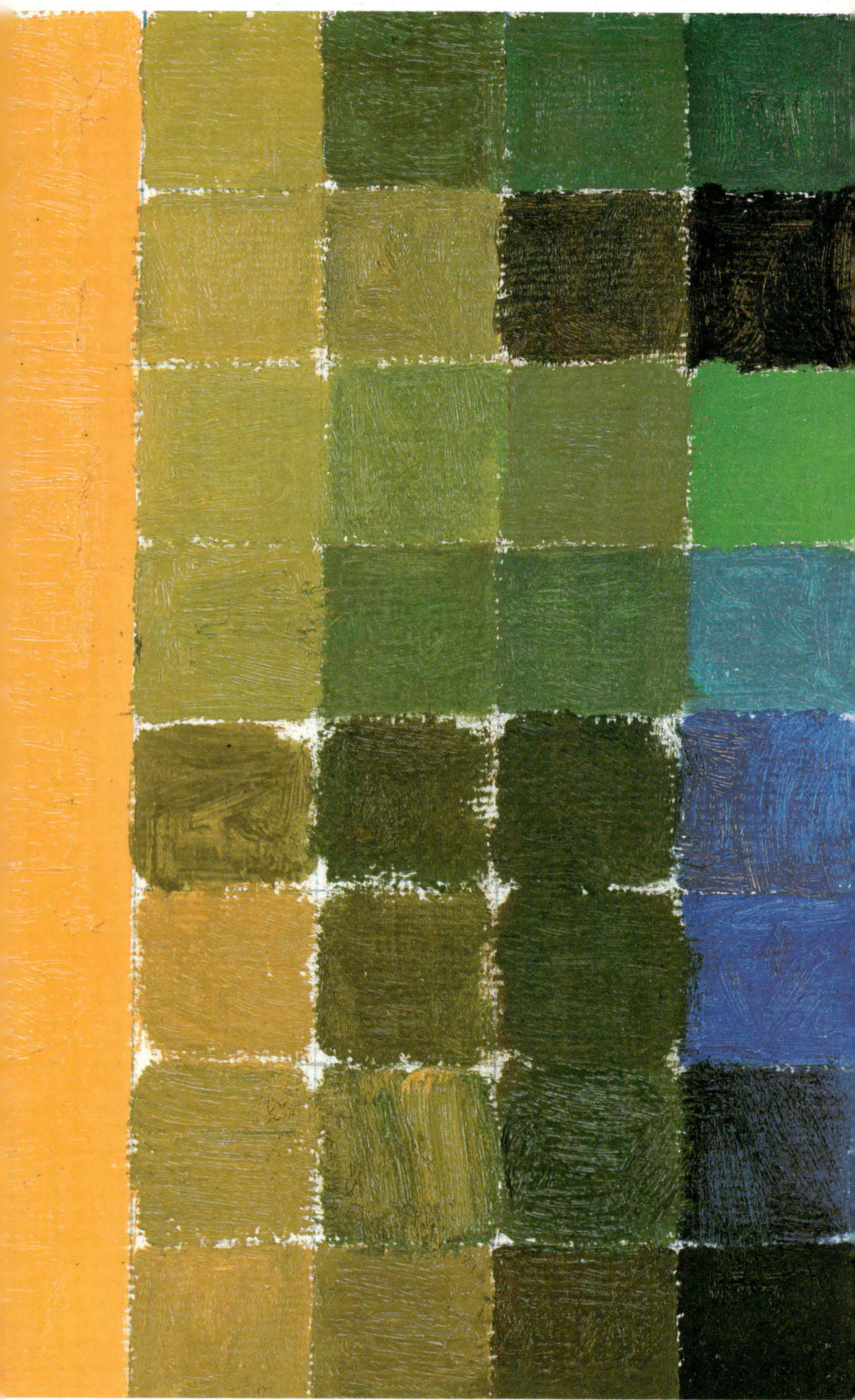

Yellow ochre	Yellow ochre 3 Cadmium red 1	Yellow ochre 2 Cadmium red 2	Yellow ochre 1 Cadmium red 3	Cadmium red
Yellow ochre	Yellow ochre 3 Alizarin crimson 1	Yellow ochre 2 Alizarin crimson 2	Yellow ochre 1 Alizarin crimson 3	Alizarin crimson
Yellow ochre	Yellow ochre 3 Light red 1	Yellow ochre 2 Light red 2	Yellow ochre 1 Light red 3	Light red
Yellow ochre	Yellow ochre 3 Venetian red 1	Yellow ochre 2 Venetian red 2	Yellow ochre 1 Venetian red 3	Venetian red
Yellow ochre	Yellow ochre 3 Raw sienna 1	Yellow ochre 2 Raw sienna 2	Yellow ochre 1 Raw sienna 3	Raw sienna
Yellow ochre	Yellow ochre 3 Burnt sienna 1	Yellow ochre 2 Burnt sienna 2	Yellow ochre 1 Burnt sienna 3	Burnt sienna
Yellow ochre	Yellow ochre 3 Raw umber 1	Yellow ochre 2 Raw umber 2	Yellow ochre 1 Raw umber 3	Raw umber
Yellow ochre	Yellow ochre 3 Burnt umber 1	Yellow ochre 2 Burnt umber 2	Yellow ochre 1 Burnt umber 3	Burnt umber

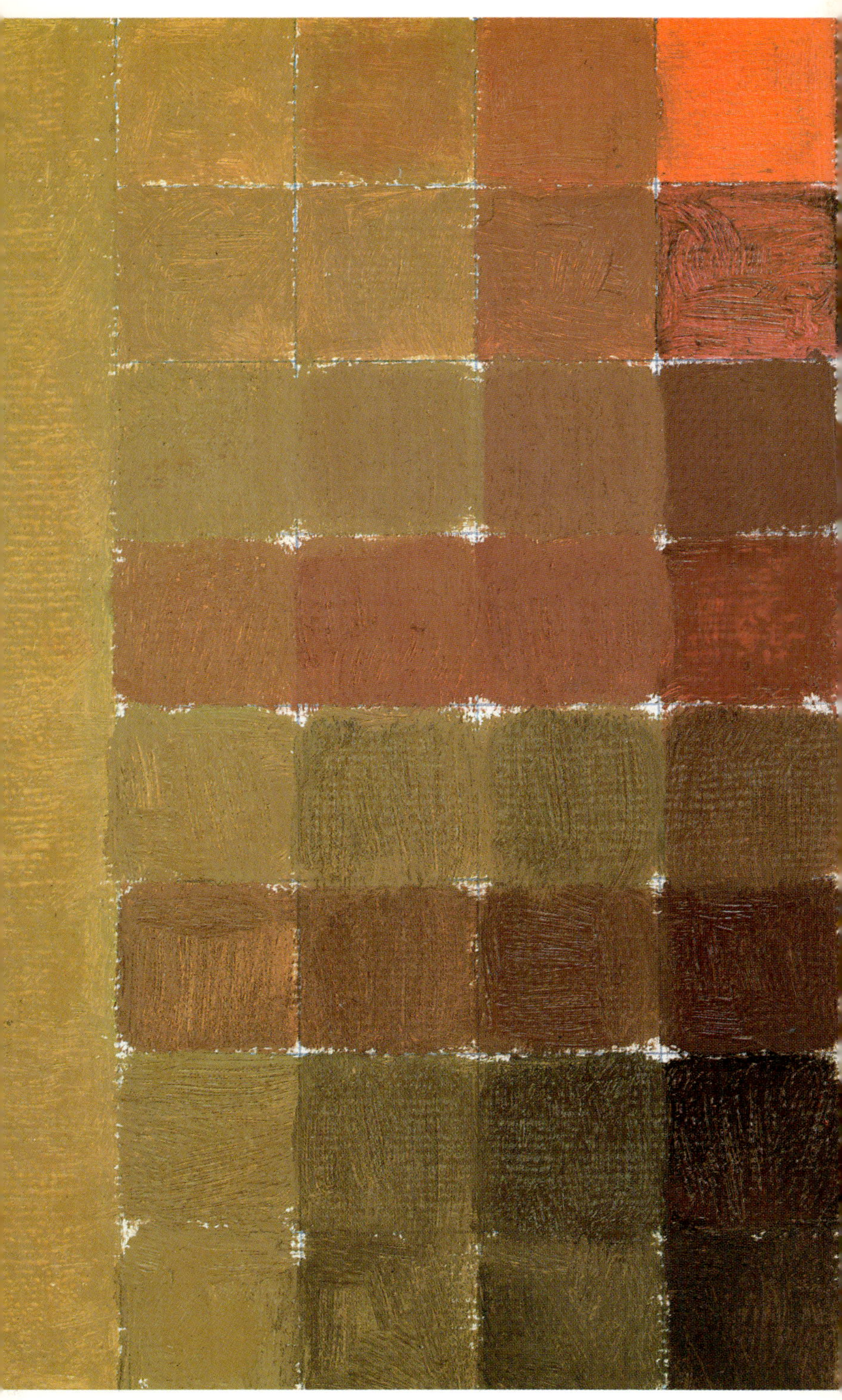

Packing up to go home

As you near the finish to your day's work, put aside a brush filled with the paint you used for the top of the picture. After you remove the clamp on your easel, you will be left with a white block of unpainted canvas. This makes a convenient carrying handle for transporting the painting with as little smudging as possible.

When you get home, fill in the space using your reserved brush; it will seldom be noticed by anyone except a fellow artist!

Finishing the actual work on a painting is by no means the end of your outing. Far from it! For me, this last period is an essential hour of personal assessment. While I tidy up my equipment and put everything away I have a chance to think about what I've accomplished and what I've learned during the day.

First, prop your painting up somewhere out of the way, but where you can continue to see it out of the corner of your eye as you move about. This works in quite an extraordinary way, as if you were taking yourself unawares. It breaks the pattern of looking directly at the picture with an intense gaze. It allows your eye to slide over the surface and to see how the paint lies on the canvas. It encourages you to glance away and back again with fresh vision.

Meanwhile, you must clean your hands or everything you touch will be dotted with paint. Use a fresh cloth and turpentine.

Then clean your brushes with turpentine. You won't get all the paint off them – do that at home in a thorough wash with soap and water – but if you wrap them in cloth they won't get hard and inflexible before you can attend to them.

If you have poured out too much turpentine, let it settle, tip the clean liquid back into the bottle and throw the rest away.

Scrape excess paint off the palette; wipe the surface with a rag and wrap it in a sheet of polythene before you put it away.

While all this is going on, you should be thinking about the day itself as well as your work. Were you warm enough, or should you have brought another sweater? Could you have done with a larger flask of coffee? Did you spend enough time on the picture, or should you have started out earlier? Was it embarrassing to work with the odd passer-by staring over your shoulder? Should you find somewhere more isolated next time? All of these externals may have influenced the way you painted as well as the quality of what you achieved.

Keep looking back at the painting while you put away all your equipment and the scraps of paper with your colour notes and sketches.

Finally, you have nothing left to pack except the painting.

This is your final chance to judge whether or not you have conveyed something of the true mood of the scene you have chosen.

This does not necessarily mean that your colours are right and the shapes accurate, although both help. It does mean that you have captured that indefinable something which makes this particular place different from another part of the landscape.

After all, the countryside is full of trees and fields, towns are full of streets and buildings. Often, one view looks very much like somewhere else. *Very* like, perhaps, but not exactly like.

And that is what you must isolate. At this moment you still have the real thing in front of you. Look at your work critically. Be honest with yourself, and with your abilities.

Now it's time to take your painting home. Never put anything on top of it. Either lay it flat on the car seat or stand it up, protected by canvas pins and two sheets of hardboard, in one of those slotted boxes made to carry wet paintings.

Be quite careful. Although the surface may seem dry, the undersurface can take quite a time to harden. If you drop an oil painting on its face, there will seldom be anything you can do to put it right again.

Home at last, prop your painting up on the mantelpiece while you make yourself a cup of coffee, and look at it again with genuine pride and pleasure. This is a moment of pure enjoyment, one of the many rewards of being an artist.

A major project

Once you begin to paint seriously in oil, you will soon feel the urge to stretch your mind and your ability by taking on a major project.

Most outdoor painters work on a fairly small scale, using boards from about 6″ (154mm) square to, say, 16″ (406mm) or 20″ (508mm) by 22″ (559mm) or 30″ (762mm). Your first venture into something larger is likely to demand a canvas twice your usual size, giving you four times the painting area.

The effort involved in such a project will be considerable, but the benefits far outweigh any of the problems you are likely to encounter. Among other simple requirements, you will be forced to use a good-sized easel, the canvas properly clamped to the top.

For the first time, perhaps, all the different points that we have touched on will have to be combined in one study. It's a bit like juggling with a set of balls; one is easy, two take a little dexterity but half a dozen require practice and training.

You will have at least six things to think about at one time, and continuously too, throughout the period – days or even weeks – that you work on the picture.

Composition suddenly becomes a different study. Instead of a conventional view of a church or a tree, you might prefer to see the spire rising in the distance against a background of rolling hills. Conversely, you might choose to sit directly under the roof or bell-tower and paint it towering into the sky above you.

The tones must be kept in mind – what sort of colour is the foreground, the middle distance, the far distance? Are you going to have a light painting, full of warm sunlight and yellow stone, or a dark green painting, touched with rich reds and purples?

When you finally come to put down your first line, it will fix the entire picture. It isn't merely the line of the horizon, or the mass of the building; it is the core around which the total composition will revolve, and it needs some thinking about, some serious consideration.

This is one case where I would always recommend that you draw in lightly what you want to see before you actually start to paint. Use a pale grey-blue, and block in a few of the basic features. Keeping it pale permits you to change your mind before you make your first firm stroke.

Now you can begin the painting itself. Working on a larger scale

you will encounter a few problems that you won't have met
before, because the dynamics of painting become quite
different.

For one thing, you will need larger brushes, otherwise you will
never be able to fill the canvas comfortably. That means more
paint, too, of course. A frequent disaster is to find yourself with
nothing left in the paint box half-way through the morning!

Concentration patterns also change. By now you should know
something about yourself as a painter – whether you do better
in half-hour stretches, breaking off for endless cups of tea and
coffee or lunch, or whether you work through the day without
stopping once your enthusiasm has been sparked.

In a major project that can take many days, you may find that
previous experiences are not necessarily a guide. The challenge
might turn a tea-break painter into a demon of concentration,
while someone normally quite happy to put in an uninterrupted
three-hour session may now want a break every half hour, if only
to stretch legs cramped with tension.

You will be reacting, in part, to pure physical facts. The canvas is
too large to work on comfortably while sitting, so you will be
forced to stand most of the time. And you won't be able to keep
the canvas directly in front of you, where it obstructs the view
you are painting; you will have to place your easel to one side,
turning either to the left or right to look at your chosen subject.

Over a longer stretch of time, the light and shadows will change
far more drastically than they do in an hour or two. If you work
slowly, you may find it sensible to come back over a period of a
week or more, arriving at roughly the same time each day, and
hoping that the weather is not too different. If it has changed
dramatically, and you find it difficult to remember what you saw
before, you may have to put your painting away for a few days
until the weather changes back again.

Don't underestimate the variations in composition that such
changing conditions can bring. Every time you put paint to
brush you can be seeing a different view!

Resign yourself to the fact that your first major painting is
unlikely to be successful. It's a huge step up from your normal
outdoor landscape, but an absolute necessity if you are to realize
your potential as an artist.

What it teaches you about yourself and the art of painting will be
more valuable than anything you have done before. Large-scale
painting should become part of your regular programme in the
coming years.

Index

Page numbers in *italic* refer to captions and illustrations.

Note on colour charts: the guides in this book have been produced within the limitations of four-colour process printing, and therefore cannot reflect the intensity of certain pure pigments.